INTRODUCTION

In the volume in this series entitled *Passenger Cars 1863-1904*, the motor-car was shown growing up, taking many shapes before the fundamentals of that which is familiar today made their appearance. This was a period of trial and error, of seeking after the most practical form for a completely new mode of transport. At first, inventors such as Sylvester Roper in the United States and Gottlieb Daimler in Germany adapted existing kinds of transport—horse-drawn carriages and bicycles—to self-propulsion by steam and gasoline. Rather later, with the German Karl Benz, the Italian Enrico Bernardi, and the Frenchmen De Dion and Bouton, the motor-car began to evolve into a machine in its own right, increasingly independent of other vehicles in its design. Being purpose-built, it worked better than the earlier compromises. It developed and survived, much as mammals did at the expense of antique dinosaurs in primeval times.

Let us look at the technological picture in 1901, taking only its most important features. Because this was a time of trial and error, variety was the rule.

This was dictated not only by lack of experience, but also by at least two other major factors. First was the suitability or otherwise of the available raw materials—metals, alloys, rubber—at a time when they had not been developed for the new industry, and when their reaction to the wholly new stresses to which they were subjected was unknown. Second and more broadly, variety was imposed by environment—

the social, economic, and geographical conditions of the different countries developing the motor vehicle. These last factors are dealt with in more detail where they belong, in the introduction to the previous volume referred to.

As well as steam and gasoline, electricity, compressed air, and other less likely forms of propulsion were used to drive the road wheels and other components. Sometimes two systems were combined in one car. Gasoline engines could be air- or water-cooled. They could be placed at the rear, centrally, or in front, and be two- or four-stroke, with one cylinder or more arranged horizontally, vertically or in vee, across or in line with the frame. Their ignition could be by hot tube or by electric spark generated by coil and battery or by low-tension magneto. Inlet valves might be automatically or mechanically actuated, and the valves disposed in the head, or overhead. There were advocates both of low-speed and of high-speed engines. Front or rear wheels might be driven. A varying number of forward speeds could be provided by belts and pulleys, by sliding-pinion gears, by the planetary system, or by friction disc. Final drive could be by belt, chain (side or central), shaft or gearing to a live or dead axle, sprung or unsprung. Steering (not necessarily of the front wheels) was achieved on the Ackermann or the centre-pivot system, with or without self-centring action, and was controlled by wheel or tiller. Either pneumatic or solid tires could be worn. The other variables were legion—flitch-plate, tubular or channel-steel frames, gilled-

I

Fig. 1. Clyde, 1908, transverse vertical three-cylinder engine

tube or honeycomb radiators in various positions, gate-type or quadrant gear-change, suspension (if there at all) independent or non-independent, by coil springs or by leaf springs in many forms (longitudinal or transverse, half-, three-quarter, or full-elliptic, or cee-spring).

However, by 1905 it could be said that the motor-car had developed into a fully independent animal, owing nothing to other forms of transport except by ancient derivation. This was truest of all outwardly. In 1900–1, the short wheelbase, high centre of gravity and body styles of the horse carriage still prevailed. With cruising speeds of 15–20 m.p.h. the rule, this hardly mattered. Now, with cruising speeds of up to double these figures and maxima of 50 or more, and the need for more comfort at those speeds, wheelbases were longer, centres of gravity lower, and wheels smaller in proportion. Bodies peculiar to the car had arisen: notably the side-entrance tourer and the formal closed limousine or landaulet. The old names like phaeton or landaulet lived on, but meant different things.

From the technical angle, basic lay-outs that worked best had been evolved to cover three types of car. The typical

Passenger Cars 1905–1912

Cars of the World in Colour

PASSENGER CARS
1905-1912

by
T. R. NICHOLSON

Illustrated by
JOHN W. WOOD
Norman Dinnage
Frank Friend
Brian Hiley
William Hobson
Tony Mitchell
Jack Pelling

LONDON
BLANDFORD PRESS

First published in 1971
Copyright © 1971 Blandford Press Ltd.
167 High Holborn, London WC1V 6PH
ISBN 0 7137 0063 7

ACKNOWLEDGMENTS

The author and the publishers are grateful to the following, who kindly read the manuscript, suggested alterations, and provided data:

From Great Britain:
E. H. Bentall Ltd.; the Bugatti Owners' Club; Mr. S. W. Darlow; Mr. Dennis and Mrs. Mary Field; Mr. G. N. Georgano; Mr. M. A. Harrison; Mr. A. R. Ronald; Mr. Michael Sedgwick; Mr. E. D. Woolley; Mr. R. J. Wyatt.

From the United States of America:
Mr. Charles L. Betts, Jr.; Mr. Jack Trefney; Dr. Alfred S. Lewerenz; Mr. Skip Marketti; Mr. Dave Rait.

From Holland:
Het Nationaal Automobielmuseum; Mr. C. Poel; Mr. S. Ten Cate.

From Switzerland:
Dr. Alfred Waldis.

From Norway:
Mr. Oluf Berrum.

From France:
Mr. Lucien Loreille.

From Australia:
Mr. G. Crittenden.

Colour section printed by Colour Reproductions Ltd, Billericay
printed in Great Britain by
Richard Clay (The Chaucer Press) Ltd, Bungay, Suffolk

larger, more powerful machine the world over would be based on the up-to-date Mercedes (10) or the rather earlier Panhard (82). It would have a water-cooled medium-speed gasoline engine at the front, with a maximum régime of about 1,000 r.p.m., four (or increasingly six) vertical cylinders cast in pairs, valves at the side, all mechanically operated by two low camshafts (the T-head layout), and ignition by low-tension magneto (or by a dual arrangement of magneto and coil and battery). In front would be a multi-tubular honeycomb radiator. A friction clutch transmitted power via a four-speed sliding-pinion gear-box and (usually) double side-chains to the rear wheels. The frame was customarily of channel-section steel, though flitch-plate frames were still seen. The half-elliptic springs were sometimes rein-forced at the rear by a single transverse spring, to help bear the formal bodies. A wheel on a raked column controlled self-centring steering, gear-change was by quadrant or gate, and the brakes were on the rear wheels and trans-mission.

The light car, or *voiturette* as it was called in France, was likely (in its European form) to vary this formula in having a high-speed engine (1,500 r.p.m.) with one or two cylinders only, coil and battery ignition, two or three forward speeds, and shaft drive to a sprung live axle. The frame was as likely to be tubular as of channel steel. In these features, it followed the De Dion Bouton (16) in its engine, and the Darracq or Renault (12, 40) as far as the complete design was concerned.

Fig. 2. De Dion drive, as used to 1911 (see 16)

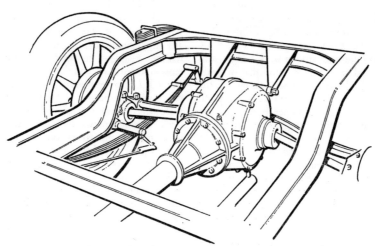

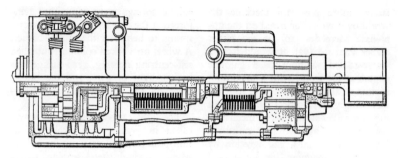

Fig. 3. 20-h.p. Lanchester, 1908, epicyclic transmission (see 30)

The American small car adhered to a low-speed, horizontal, centrally-mounted engine with one or two large cylinders, planetary (epicyclic) gearing, drive by central chain, and suspension by a single longitudinal leaf spring on each side which did the duty of frame members as well: the 'gas-buggy' formula.

Changes in the seven years covered in this book were few. Closed bodywork for formal town use was conservative by nature, and changed little. The driver was given a roof over his head, and more usually, in 1912, had a windshield in front of him; that was all. Only this type of body was closed: the popular sedan was still a long way off. From about 1909 open bodywork was in transition, losing the curvilinear *art nouveau* opulence of 1905, which had its attraction, and progressing by exceedingly awkward stages towards the simple, clean elegance of the 'torpedo' style of the succeeding age, with its flush top line of hood, scuttle and body sides, and lack of excrescences anywhere.

Mechanically, too, one trend was towards simplification and rationalization, in the interests of cheapness and efficiency—a movement made possible by advances in metallurgy and electrical technology. Among the large cars steps were being taken towards replacing bibloc with monobloc casting of cylinders, which permitted shorter, stiffer crankshafts and higher revolutions even if the standard of casting was not at first so high. The L-head valve layout, with a single camshaft operating all valves, which were now all on one side, gradually supplanted the T-head. The high-tension magneto replaced the low-tension instrument, and shaft drive to a live axle (almost as invariably) the side-chains of an earlier age. Chassis frames were nearly always of channel-section steel. Engine speeds increased most noticeably in the larger type of car, 1,500 r.p.m. now being normal. Anything over 2,000 r.p.m. was exceptional.

Another trend was towards refinement, under which heading we may include silence, smoothness, flexibility, and ease of control, and which was most noticeable in this class of car, whose owners could afford the price of such luxuries. This was the first great age of the six-cylinder engine (17, 20) and of the sleeve valve (82, 94)—the products of the endless search for the first three qualities mentioned. The gate gear-change supplanted the progressive quadrant, being easier to operate and allowing more flexible handling of the car. Apart from its other advantages, the monobloc engine produced its power more smoothly than the bi-bloc (or, *a fortiori*, the engine with separately cast cylinders), thanks to its shorter crankshaft. A further trend most noticeable in the big car was in the direction of more power obtained more smoothly thanks to more and bigger cylinders; but engine efficiency, in terms of the ratio of power output to engine size, was improving too. The Mercedes of 1901, the paragon of its day, gave 35 b.h.p. from nearly six litres, and the contemporary $4\frac{1}{2}$-h.p. De Dion Bouton the indicated output from half a litre. Drawing comparisons, the Chevrolet Classic Six of 1912, with 4·8 litres, offered 50 b.h.p.; the 2·6-litre 12 CV Métallurgique provided 32 b.h.p. in 1910; and the 1912 Fiat Tipo Zero, of 1·8 litres, produced 19 b.h.p. Thus 6–9 b.h.p. per litre had improved to 10–12 b.h.p. per litre in ten years.

Growing refinement was perceptible also, in Europe, in new offerings of the old type of twin-cylinder small car; even in those that were low-priced, such as the Renault Model AX (40), the 10/12-h.p. Alldays (42), the 8-h.p. Humber (41), and the Jowett (70). But refinement in light cars was due much more to their increasing adoption of the characteristics of their bigger brethren: multicylinder engines of modern de-sign, high-tension magneto ignition, a honeycomb radiator, gate change, channel-steel frames. The true 'big-car-in-miniature' beloved of European motorists of limited means to this day was not yet universal in 1912: although exceptions such as the Le Zèbre (64), a real 'teuf-teuf' in the delightful French phrase, were still popular, its day was only just about to dawn, and the precursors had come: Morris-Oxford (89), Clément-Bayard Type 4M (66), Opel 4/8 PS (50), Adler 6/14 PS (59), Stoewer Typ B2 (60). Meanwhile some makers, especially in Britain, were taking another road into the ultra-light field, Riley and AC (44, 55) had started life as simple tricycles one stage more desir-able than a motor-cycle, but in our period developed their products into comfortable, fast, highly successful little tricars and before (or just after) the end of it, went over to four wheels.

The small car's American counter-part paid the penalty of excessive con-servatism. It did not so much develop as die, suddenly; although in its time it had spread across the Atlantic (the Oldsmobile was very popular in Britain, which even produced, in the shape of the Adams (29), an 'imitation' American gas-buggy). The age of the gas-buggy was well and truly over by 1912, by which time the American public did not want small cars in any shape or form: they wanted the space and comfort of the big car, and as soon as Henry Ford provided it (47) for the price (or for less than the price) of a machine of the older sort, the latter was doomed. The twin-cylinder Maxwell (23), one of the best of the breed, lasted until 1912; the little Brush runabout (57) until 1913. From 1909, too, Buick

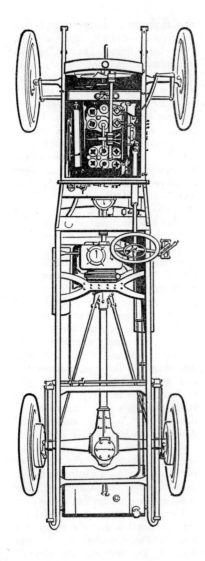

Fig. 4. Mercedes 8/18 PS, 1909, plan view of chassis. Classic shaft-drive layout

made only multicylinder cars (74). The popular American economy car of 1912 is exemplified not only by the 2·9-litre Ford Model T, but by the machines called into existence to compete with it by offering more amenities at a higher price—such as the Buick 15/20 h.p. of 2·7 litres (74), and the K.R.I.T. of 2·9 litres (90), both fours. Apart from their low price, which in turn meant simplicity exemplified by two-speed epicyclic gears (which endured on many cars until the end of the period), coil and battery ignition, a certain starkness of décor and a relative slowness in adopting the most modern technical features (see below), these machines differed hardly at all in their fundamentals from the European big car.

In America as in Europe, momentous events were casting their shadows before in this period. The motor-car in Europe, while no longer exclusively a rich man's toy, was still very much a convenience, if not a luxury, for the better-off middle classes. It was the day of the 'Doctor's Coupé', not of the Volkswagen. The same was true of the United States, but the revolution which was to put a car into the hands of every seventh person (or about every second family) by 1929 was much nearer. The mass assembly of a standardized product with interchangeable and therefore accurately made parts was not new, having been applied under the exigency of war to the manufacture of pulley-blocks and guns in Britain and the United States a century before, and to pocket-watch manufacture in the latter country since then. De Dion, Bouton et Cie applied it to car parts in the 1890s, making 20,000 engines between 1895 and 1901, and 1,500 complete cars in

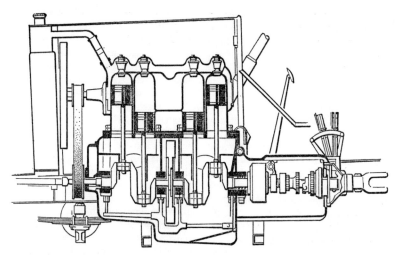

Fig. 5. Motobloc four-cylinder 2½-litre engine, *en bloc* with gear-box, central flywheel

their first two years of production (1899–1901). Alexandre Darracq, also in France, built over 1,200 cars in 1901. In the United States, Henry Leland supplied engines made to such standards to Ford's first enterprises, the Detroit Automobile Company and the Henry Ford Company, both of which failed, and to Ransom E. Olds for his Oldsmobile, of which 2,500 were built in 1902 and twice as many in 1904. 1,500 Ramblers were sold in 1902, and when Leland turned to car manufacture, he produced 1,700 Model A Cadillacs in 1903–4. When Ford tried again with his Ford Motor Company, he made more than that total in 1903 alone.

However, although all these manufacturers achieved low prices in comparison with most obtaining before, the mass market which could allow the new methods full scope and reduce costs fantastically, was not yet there. It first opened up in America, where by the end of our period the state of the roads, which had earlier faced the motorist with an obstacle he seldom met in Europe, was improving slowly thanks to the agitation first of the cycling fraternity, then of the railway interests (who saw a bright future for the motorcar as a feeder), and finally of the growing company of motorists themselves: nearly two million by 1914. Road improvement meant a greater demand for cars, so the process fed on itself.

Another very new development was that, as we have seen, design had settled down enough to allow a manufacturer safely to tool up for a long run of what would necessarily be a standardized

7

product: fashion was not, it seemed, changing at the same rate as before. Furthermore, the product was commending itself to more and more people not only because there were beginning to be roads to drive it on, but also because it was now normally a reliable, untemperamental animal that could be made easy for the layman to control.

There were several conditions that already existed to favour the coming of true mass-production in the United States. One was the existence of a very large and prosperous class working in, or deriving its income from, industry that would buy a car if it were made cheap and otherwise desirable enough. The market was there. Another was the fact that these people included relatively few workmen with the high degree of skill needed for hand-finishing of parts according to the traditional methods of car manufacture, which were in any case very slow and expensive; potent discouragements to the production of large numbers of cheap vehicles by these methods. On the other hand, the technical knowhow existed among American engineers (as elsewhere) to invent, once the impulse was there, the specialized machine tools required to make plant able to turn out at high speed parts tailored to precisely standardized specification. At the same time, a vast pool of unskilled labour existed, which could be turned to minding and feeding the new machines.

Henry Ford and his backers were the first to recognize the combined force of the new trends and the existing conditions, and to take advantage of it. Their vision was to give Ford a stranglehold on the low-priced market for twenty years. The Ford Model T of 1909 (47) was the cheapest four-cylinder car available, at $825, rendering the Maxwell twin and its like a drug on the market. Ford's gamble in pricing his new car so low, and his preparedness to take advantage of the demand he would thus create, paid off. He sold 11,000 Model Ts in 1908–9, the first year of production. Such sales were not only justified, but also demanded by his methods.

At the same time, true mass-production did not come until after the end of the era described in this book. It did so only with the arrival of the moving assembly line, which was not to be adopted by Ford until 1913, and then only, at first, for his flywheel generators. His competitors followed, as usual. In 1912 and earlier, cheapness was obtainable through long production runs, but they took longer to sell, because until a mass market developed, sales were slower. Massive retooling was necessary if, for instance, one was to go over to making one's own engines monobloc instead of bi-bloc. Such changes were extremely expensive in plant, and could not be contemplated until the current investment had justified itself. Thus, any cars—not exclusively American ones—built on these principles tended to lag behind the go-ahead small producer in technical sophistication. Because even now, United States production was bigger than that of other countries, and its products cheaper and widely diffused abroad, this conservatism was especially obtrusive in American vehicles. Europe, conversely, could still afford to specialize in shorter runs of generally more advanced, better appointed, and much more expensive machines in the economy-car sphere. It should be recalled, however, that when American cars were modern in design, no one could surpass them in this. A good example was the 30-h.p. Chalmers-Detroit of 1909 (48), with its overhead-valve, short-stroke, high-speed mono-bloc engine.

What has gone before is generalization; there were, in this period, plenty of other exceptions, on both sides of the Atlantic. In the United States, steam was a strong contender until the end of the era. The simple steamers of Stanley were built until the middle 1920s, while the more complicated and sophisticated White survived as a steamer until 1911. The advantages of steam *vis-à-vis* the gasoline car—silence, lack of fumes, flexibility, smoothness, acceleration—still outweighed its disadvantages of relative complication and lengthy starting routine. However, the advent of the electric self-starter in 1912, initially on Leland's Cadillacs, must have accelerated the steamer's decline. Electricity as a source of motive power hardly counts, since it was never popular for anything but town use by the wealthy, the limiting factors being the range of its batteries, and the specialized and therefore expensive maintenance required. With few exceptions (26), electric cars (and even taxicabs) were dead in Europe soon after the turn of the century, though retaining their attraction for the dowager market in America throughout the 1920s. Indeed, the Detroit Electric Car Company made cars to order as late as 1942. Electricity as an auxiliary source of power in Europe lasted longer (see CIEM, later Stella, 96).

Among gasoline-engined cars, the 'high-wheeler' (22, 32) was a vehicle peculiar to this period, blooming briefly in response to the specialized needs of the Middle Western farmer-motorist before they became catered for more conventionally by Ford. In Germany, the spiritual home of the big, powerful, and orthodox, there flourished beside the Mercedes (10), the Benz (58), the NAG (11) and the Rex-Simplex (92), the Phänomobil (61) and the Piccolo (15); two vehicles with which, in different ways, it would be hard to find parallels in any other country,

Fig. 6. Valveless engine cycle (see 56)

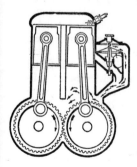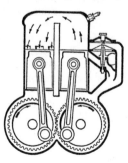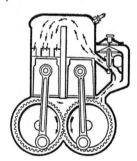

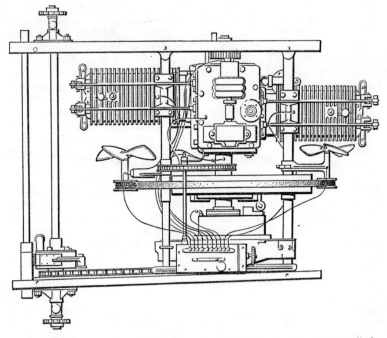

Fig. 7. I.H.C., 1911. Plan of running gear. Transverse horizontal two-cylinder
air-cooled engine (see 22)

let alone Germany. Most surprising of all, the Phänomobil, one of the strangest creations to emerge from any car factory anywhere, did so with considerable *élan* for twenty years, outliving many of its conventional contemporaries. The 17 CV Panhard-Levassor of 1912 (82) could combine in one car the modernity and refinement of Mr Charles Yale Knight's sleeve valves with the nineteenth-century crudity of a flitch-plate frame. Air-cooling, like steam and electricity, had a longer run in America than in Europe, and the Franklin (73) was current until 1934.

This was still a time when a small-scale works with its own, or convenient, foundry facilities and a few low-paid skilled hand-craftsmen could economically make and sell (usually locally) a handful of cars at a time at a high price, especially if they were backed by other established lines such as agricultural machinery, commercial vehicles, railway rolling-stock, etc. In this class were the makers of the Bentall (31), Stella (96), Scania (80), Cottereau (2), and myriad others. Public taste was not yet so standardized that the products of such concerns could not be of unusual design in some respects—for example, the superb Lanchester (30), the two-stroke Cooper (43) and Valveless (56), and the even odder Compound (14).

Equally small firms flourished now, and long after (so long as they were prepared to accept technical orthodoxy) by assembling cars from parts bought out from specialist manufacturers of the more complex components, that could not be readily run up in any workshop. The latter had flourished ever since De Dion, Bouton et Cie, best known as makers of complete cars, had built up an exceedingly profitable line in engines as well, as we have seen. Henry M. Leland sold engines to Oldsmobile and Ford and the Dodge brothers sold gear-boxes to the same customers. Engines came from Aster, Buchet, Ballot, White & Poppe; Longuemare made carburettors; Simms-Bosch provided magnetos; radiators, gear-boxes, and rear-axle units came from yet other addresses. Even simple items such as chassis frames could be bought 'off the peg', from Cottereau of Dijon (2) among others. In the end, the assemblers as a tribe outlived the small manufacturers, as their plant costs and overheads were lower; but they tended to be ephemeral, as they depended upon suppliers whose stocks, prices, standards, and reliability generally could be variable. Generally speaking, too, the quality of their products tended to vary more than that of cars manufactured entirely by one firm,

Fig. 8. 15-h.p. Napier, 1912, engine. Classic bi-bloc unit

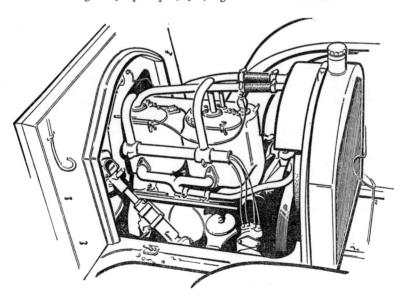

since they were essentially patchwork creations which could be and often were very carefully put together, but sometimes were not. At the same time, the range of proprietary parts available was so great that although assembled cars shared a basic orthodoxy, they could be put together in almost limitless permutations, preserving fair individuality of character.

So, one way and another, it can be seen that this was a time of considerable variety and interest, in spite of the basic and accelerating tendency for design to settle down. It was a highly important transitional period between the fascinating technological anarchy of the previous age and the conformity of the next, which was to be illumined not by the technical interest of the vehicles themselves—very much the reverse, as far as passenger cars were concerned—but by the historic importance of the methods used to produce and sell them, and of the effects of their first massed invasion of society.

AUTHOR'S NOTES

The dates given to the cars painted are usually of the particular vehicles illustrated, or, if the precise date is unknown, of the currency of the model. A reference to the descriptive text under 'Passenger Cars in Detail' (p. 109–159) will tell the reader which applies.

The colouring of a car as shown is not necessarily that in which it was normally seen or catalogued. It has been dictated by the exigencies of an attractive page layout. In many instances, though, cars were to be seen, if not catalogued, in almost any colour, since this could be at the discretion of the buyer (particularly in the cases of custom-built bodies).

For the sake of interest and to provide an idea of the variety to be seen on the basic model, different body styles, etc. are illustrated, even if unusual, i.e. they are not necessarily representative. Any two views of one car are not necessarily to scale; nor are the views of different cars on the same or adjoining pages.

Approximate conversion of cylinder bore and stroke: 25·4 millimetres (mm.) = 1 inch.

Approximate conversion of engine cubic capacity: 16·4 cubic centimetres (c.c.) = 1 cubic inch.

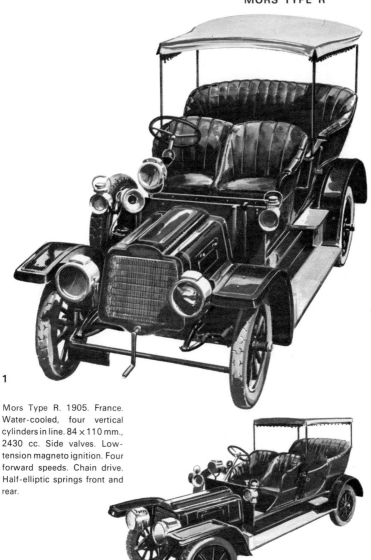

1

Mors Type R. 1905. France. Water-cooled, four vertical cylinders in line. 84 × 110 mm., 2430 cc. Side valves. Low-tension magneto ignition. Four forward speeds. Chain drive. Half-elliptic springs front and rear.

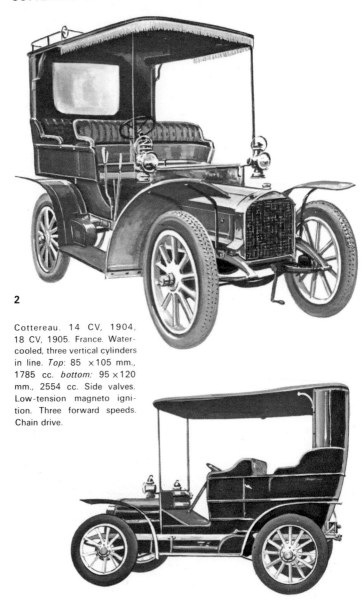

2

Cottereau. 14 CV, 1904, 18 CV, 1905. France. Water-cooled, three vertical cylinders in line. *Top*: 85 × 105 mm., 1785 cc. *bottom:* 95 × 120 mm., 2554 cc. Side valves. Low-tension magneto ignition. Three forward speeds. Chain drive.

3

Mass 8 CV. 1905. France, Water-cooled, single vertical cylinder, 100 × 120 mm., 942 cc. Automatic inlet valve. Battery and coil ignition. Three forward speeds. Shaft drive. Half-elliptic springs front and rear, auxiliary transverse spring at rear.

VAUXHALL 9 H.P.

4

Vauxhall 9 h.p. 1905. Great Britain. Water-cooled, three vertical cylinders in line. 80 × 110 mm., 1675 cc. Side valves. Coil and battery ignition. Three forward speeds. Chain drive. Half-elliptic springs front and rear.

5

Daimler 30 h.p., 1906, 35 h.p., 1905. Great Britain. Water-cooled, four vertical cylinders in line. *Top:* 125 × 150 mm., 7247 cc.; *bottom:* 134 × 150 mm., 8462 cc. Side valves. High-tension magneto or coil ignition. Four forward speeds. Chain drive. Half-elliptic springs front and rear.

ROLLS ROYCE 15 H.P.

Rolls Royce 15 h.p. 1905. Great Britain. Water-cooled, three vertical cylinders in line. 100 × 127 mm., 3000 cc. Overhead inlet valves, side exhaust valves. High-tension magneto and coil ignition. Three forward speeds. Shaft drive. Half-elliptic springs front and rear, auxiliary transverse spring at rear.

7

Craig-Dorwald S-Type. 1905. Great Britain. Four vertical cylinders in line. 127 × 140 mm., 7100 cc. Side valves. Coil and low-tension magneto ignition. Three forward speeds. Chain drive.

PIERCE GREAT ARROW 28 H.P.

8

Pierce Great Arrow 28 h.p. 1905. U.S.A. Water-cooled, four vertical cylinders in line. 108 × 121 mm., 4436 cc. Side valves. High-tension magneto and coil ignition. Three forward speeds. Shaft drive. Half-elliptic springs front and rear.

9

Peerless 35 h.p., 1905, 24 h.p., 1904. U.S.A. Water-cooled, four vertical cylinders in line. *Top:* 117 × 140 mm., 6023 cc.; *bottom:* 108 × 102 mm., 3720 cc. Side valves. Low-tension magneto and coil ignition. *Top:* Three forward speeds; *bottom:* four forward speeds. Shaft drive. Half-elliptic springs front and rear.

10

Mercedes 35/40 PS. 1906, 1905. Germany. Water-cooled, four vertical cylinders in line. 110 × 140 mm., 5320 cc. Low-tension magneto ignition. Four forward speeds. Chain drive. Half-elliptic springs front and rear.

11

NAG 20/24 PS. 1906, 1905. Germany. Water-cooled, four vertical cylinders in line. 115 × 125 mm., 5200 cc. Side valves. Low-tension magneto ignition. Four forward speeds. Chain drive. Three-quarter-elliptic front springs, half-elliptic rear springs.

RENAULT 20/30 CV

12

Renault 20/30 CV. 1906. France. Water-cooled, four vertical cylinders in line. 100 ×140 mm., 4398 cc. Side valves in L head. High-tension magneto ignition. Four forward speeds. Shaft drive. Half-elliptic springs front and rear, auxiliary transverse spring at rear.

13

Albion A6. 1906, 1910. Great Britain. Water-cooled, four vertical cylinders in line. 108 × 114 mm., 4180 cc. Side valves. Low-tension magneto ignition. Four forward speeds. Chain final drive. Half-elliptic front springs, full-elliptic rear springs.

COMPOUND 12/15 H.P.

Compound 12/15 h.p. 1906. U.S.A. Water-cooled, three vertical cylinders in line. 102 × 102 mm., 1668 cc. (high-pressure cylinders), 178 × 102 mm., 2539 cc. (low-pressure cylinder). Side valves. Coil and battery ignition. Three forward speeds. Shaft or chain drive. Half-elliptic springs front and rear.

15

Piccolo 5 PS. 1906. Germany. Air-cooled, two cylinders in vee formation. 75 × 80 mm., 704 cc. Side valves. Coil and battery ignition. Two forward speeds. Shaft drive. Half-elliptic springs front and rear.

DE DION-BOUTON TYPE AV

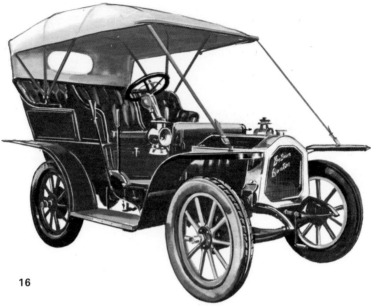

16

De Dion-Bouton Type AV. 1908, 1907. France. Water-cooled, two vertical cylinders in line. 80 × 120 mm., 1204 cc. Side valves. Battery and coil ignition. Three forward speeds. Shaft drive. Half-elliptic springs front and rear.

17

Rolls Royce 40/50 h.p. 1907. Great Britain. Water-cooled, six vertical cylinders in line. 114 x 114 mm., 7036 cc. Side valves. High-tension magneto and trembler coil ignition. Four forward speeds. Shaft drive. Half-elliptic springs front and rear (to late 1907), auxiliary transverse spring at rear.

STANDARD 30 H.P., 40 H.P.

18

Standard 30 h.p., 1907, 40 h.p., 1910. Great Britain. Water-cooled, six vertical cylinders in line. *Top:* 102 × 108 mm., 5300 cc.; *bottom:* 102 × 127 mm., 6225 cc. Coil or high-tension magneto ignition. Four forward speeds. Shaft drive. Half-elliptic front springs, full-elliptic rear springs.

19

New Eagle. 1907, 1908. Great
Britain. Water-cooled, four
vertical cylinders in line. Side
valves. Three forward speeds.
Epicyclic gears. Shaft drive.
Three quarter-elliptic front
springs, full-elliptic rear
springs.

NAPIER 45 H.P., 40 H.P.

20

Napier 45 h.p. 1908, 40 h.p.
1907. Great Britain. Water-
cooled, six vertical cylinders
in line. *Top:* 102 × 127 mm.,
6160 cc.; *bottom:* 102 × 102
mm., 4940 cc. Side valves.
High-tension magneto ignition. Three forward speeds.
Shaft drive. Half-elliptic
springs front and rear.

21

Thomas Flyer Model 6-70. 1907. U.S.A. Water-cooled, six vertical cylinders in line. 140 × 140 mm., 12936 cc. Side valves. High-tension magneto ignition. Four forward speeds. Chain drive. Half-elliptic springs front and rear.

22

I.H.C. 1907. U.S.A. Air-cooled, two horizontal cylinders. 127 × 127 mm., 3216 cc. Overhead valves. Coil and battery ignition. Two forward speeds. Epicyclic gears. Chain drive. Full-elliptic springs front and rear.

23

Maxwell Model H.B. 1907, Model A. 1909. U.S.A. Water-cooled, two horizontal cylinders. *Top:* 127 ×127 mm., 3219 cc. ; *bottom:* 102 ×102 mm., 1668 cc. Side valves. High-tension magneto ignition. Three forward speeds. Shaft drive. *Top:* half-elliptic springs front and rear; *bottom:* full-elliptic springs front and rear.

LAURIN-KLEMENT TYPE B

24

Laurin-Klement Type B. 1907, 1908. Austria-Hungary (Bohemia). Water-cooled, two cylinders in vee formation. 90 × 100 mm., 1400 cc. Overhead inlet valves, side exhaust valves. High-tension magneto and coil ignition. Three forward speeds. Shaft drive. Half-elliptic springs front and rear.

25

Itala 35/45 h.p. 1907. Italy. Water-cooled, four vertical cylinders in line. 130 × 140 mm., 7433 cc. Side valves. Low-tension magneto ignition. Four forward speeds. Shaft drive. Half-elliptic springs front and rear.

26

Tribelhorn Phaeton 1908, Victoria 1907. Switzerland. Electric. *See text for available details.*

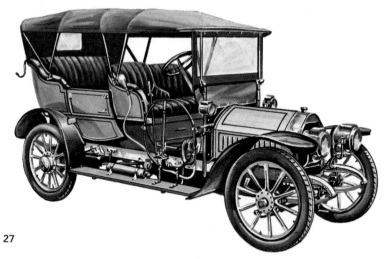

27

Peugeot 16 h.p., Type 116, 1908, 7/9 h.p., Type 125, 1911. France. Water-cooled. *Top:* four vertical cylinders in line; *bottom:* two cylinders in line. *Top:* 80 × 110 mm., 2211 cc.; *bottom:* 75 × 130 mm., 1149 cc. Side valves. High-tension magneto ignition. *Top:* four forward speeds; *bottom:* three forward speeds. Shaft drive. Half-elliptic springs front and rear.

BRASIER TYPE VL

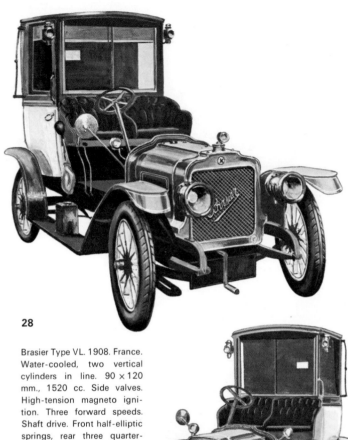

28

Brasier Type VL. 1908. France.
Water-cooled, two vertical
cylinders in line. 90 × 120
mm., 1520 cc. Side valves.
High-tension magneto ignition. Three forward speeds.
Shaft drive. Front half-elliptic
springs, rear three quarter-
elliptic springs.

29

Adams 10 h.p. 1908. Great Britain. Water-cooled, single horizontal cylinder. 121 × 152 mm., 1750 cc. Side valves. Battery and coil, or high-tension magneto ignition. Three forward speeds. Epicyclic gears. Chain final drive. Suspension: Single full-length spring each side, or front three-quarter elliptic springs and rear full elliptic springs.

30

Lanchester 20 h.p. 1908. Great Britain. Water-cooled, four vertical cylinders in line. 102 × 76 mm., 2485 cc. Horizontal overhead valves. High-tension magneto ignition. Three forward speeds. Epicyclic gears. Shaft drive. Cantilever springs front and rear.

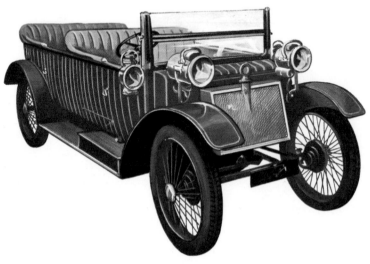

31

Bentall 16/20 h.p. 1908. Great Britain. Water-cooled, four vertical cylinders in line. 100 × 95 mm., 2984 cc. Side valves. High-tension magneto ignition. Three forward speeds. Shaft drive. Front half-elliptic springs, rear full-elliptic springs.

SCHACHT

32

Schacht. 1908. U.S.A. Water-cooled, two horizontal cylinders. 102 × 102 mm., 1600 cc. Side valves. Coil and battery ignition. Infinitely variable friction-disc transmission. Chain drive. Single full-length spring each side.

33

White 30 h.p. 1908. U.S.A. Steam engine. Compound, double-acting. Two vertical cylinders. Flash generator. Kerosene burner. Shaft drive.

STEARNS 45/90 H.P.

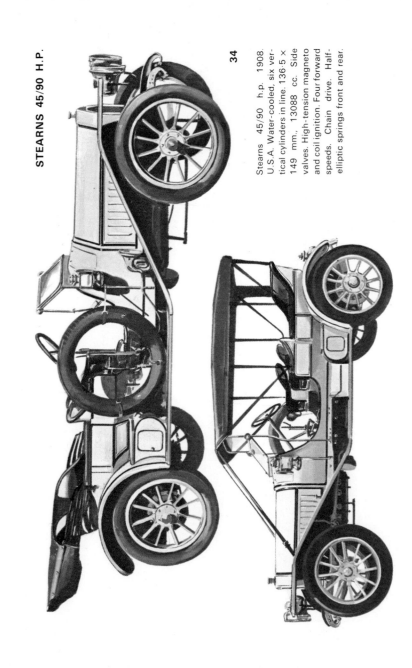

34

Stearns 45/90 h.p. 1908. U.S.A. Water-cooled, six vertical cylinders in line. 136·5 × 149 mm, 13088 cc. Side valves. High-tension magneto and coil ignition. Four forward speeds. Chain drive. Half-elliptic springs front and rear.

35

Gaggenau Typ 60, 1907, Typ D10-18, 1908. Germany. Water-cooled, four vertical cylinders in line. *Top:* 125 × 180 mm., 8830 cc., single overhead camshaft; *bottom:* 85 × 115 mm., 2600 cc., side valves. High-tension magneto and coil ignition. *Top:* four forward speeds; *bottom:* three or four forward speeds. *Top:* chain drive; *bottom:* shaft drive. Half-elliptic springs front and rear.

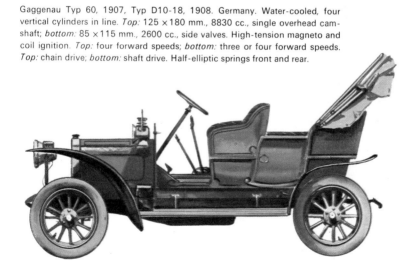

LANCIA TIPO 51 ALFA

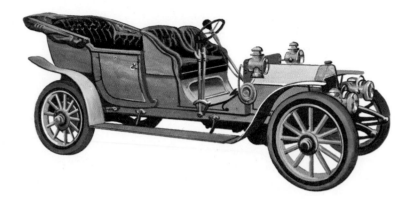

36

Lancia Tipo 51 Alfa. 1908. Italy. Water-cooled, four vertical cylinders in line. 90 × 100 mm., 2546 cc. Side valves. High-tension magneto ignition. Four forward speeds. Shaft drive. Front half-elliptic springs, rear three-quarter-elliptic springs.

37

Fiat 18/24 h.p. 1908. Italy. Water-cooled, four vertical cylinders in line. 105 × 130 mm., 4500 cc. Side valves. High-tension magneto ignition. Four forward speeds. Chain drive. Half-elliptic springs front and rear.

GERMAIN 18/22 H.P.

38

Germain 18/22 h.p. 1908. Belgium. Water-cooled, four vertical cylinders in line. 102 × 110 mm., 3598 cc. Side valves. High-tension magneto ignition. Three forward speeds. Shaft drive. Half-elliptic front springs, three-quarter-elliptic rear springs.

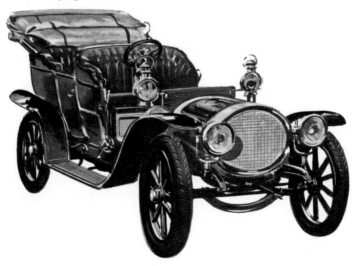

39

Ajax 8/16 CV. 1908. Switzerland. Water-cooled, four vertical cylinders in line. 85 × 100 mm., 2270 cc. Side valves. High-tension magneto ignition. Four forward speeds. Shaft drive. Half-elliptic springs front and rear.

RENAULT MODEL AX

40

Renault Model AX. 1909.
France. Water-cooled, two
vertical cylinders in line. 75 ×
120 mm., 1060 cc. Side valves.
High-tension magneto ignition. Three forward speeds.
Shaft drive. Half-elliptic
springs front and rear.

41

Humber 8 h.p. 1909. Great Britain. Water-cooled, two vertical cylinders in line. 90 × 120 mm., 1525 cc. Side valves. High-tension magneto and coil ignition. Three forward speeds. Shaft drive. Half-elliptic springs front and rear.

ALLDAYS & ONIONS 10/12 H.P.

42

Alldays & Onions 10/12 h.p. 1909. Great Britain. Water-cooled, two vertical cylinders in line. 95 × 114 mm., 1630 cc. Side valves. High-tension magneto ignition. Three forward speeds. Shaft drive. Half-elliptic springs front and rear.

43

Cooper. 1909. Great Britain. Water-cooled, four vertical cylinders in line. 95 × 114 mm., 3260 cc. Two-stroke, piston valves. High-tension magneto ignition. Three forward speeds, two-speed axle. Shaft drive. Half-elliptic front springs, unequal cantilever and transverse rear springs.

RILEY 10 H.P.

44

Riley 10 h.p. 1909. Great Britain. Water-cooled, two cylinders in vee formation. 96 × 96 mm., 1388 cc. Side valves. High-tension magneto and coil
ignition. Three forward speeds. Shaft drive. Half-elliptic springs front and rear.

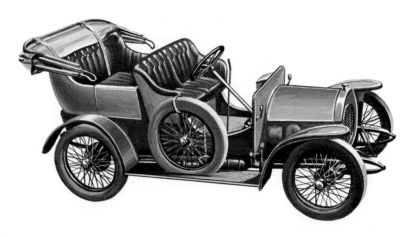

45

Austin 7 h.p. 1909. Great
Britain. Water-cooled, single
vertical cylinder. 105 × 127
mm., 1087 cc. Side valves.
High-tension magneto or coil
ignition. Three forward speeds.
Shaft drive. Front half-elliptic
springs, rear three-quarter-
elliptic springs.

VAUXHALL 12/16 H.P.

46

Vauxhall 12/16 h.p. 1909. Great Britain. Water-cooled, four vertical cylinders in line. 80 × 110 mm., 2212 cc. Side valves. High-tension magneto ignition. Three forward speeds. Shaft drive. Half-elliptic springs front and rear.

47

Ford Model T. 1909. U.S.A. Water-cooled, four vertical cylinders in line. 95 × 102 mm., 2894 cc. Side valves. Flywheel magneto and coil ignition. Two forward speeds, epicyclic gears. Shaft drive. Transverse half-elliptic springs front and rear.

48

Chalmers-Detroit Model F. 1909. U.S.A. Water-cooled, four vertical cylinders in line. 102 × 114 mm., 3727 cc. Pushrod-operated overhead valves. Coil and battery or high-tension magneto ignition. Three forward speeds. Shaft drive. Half-elliptic springs front and rear.

49

Premier 40 h.p. 1909, 1910. U.S.A. Water-cooled, four vertical cylinders in line. 114 × 133 mm., 5432 cc. Side valves. High-tension magneto and coil ignition. Three forward speeds. Shaft drive. Full-elliptic springs front and rear.

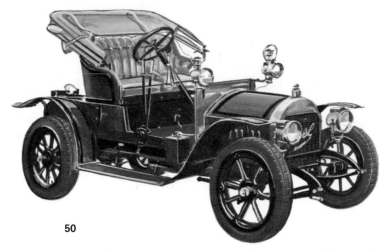

50

Opel 4/8 PS. 1909. Germany. Water-cooled, four vertical cylinders in line. 64 × 85 mm., 1128 cc. Side valves. High-tension magneto ignition. Three forward speeds. Shaft drive. Half-elliptic springs front and rear.

51

Martini 12/16 CV. 1909, 1911. Switzerland. Water-cooled, four vertical cylinders in line. 80 × 110 mm., 2212 cc. Overhead inlet, side exhaust valves. High-tension magneto ignition. Four forward speeds. Shaft drive. Half-elliptic springs front and rear.

52

Delaunay-Belleville Type HB, 1911, Type H, 1910. France. Water-cooled, six vertical cylinders in line. *Top:* 85 × 130 mm., 4426 cc.; *bottom:* 85 × 120 mm., 4087 cc. Side valves. High-tension magneto ignition. Four forward speeds. Shaft drive. Half-elliptic springs front and rear, auxiliary transverse spring at rear.

53

Hotchkiss Type T. 1910. France. Water-cooled, four vertical cylinders in line. 95 × 110 mm., 3120 cc. Side valves, high-tension magneto ignition. Four forward speeds. Shaft drive. Front half-elliptic springs, rear three-quarter-elliptic springs.

DEASY 12 H.P.

54

Deasy 12 h.p. 1910. Great Britain. Water-cooled, four vertical cylinders in line. 75 × 110 mm., 1944 cc. Side valves. High-tension magneto ignition. Three or four forward speeds. Shaft drive. Half-elliptic front springs, three-quarter-elliptic rear springs.

55

AC Sociable. 1910. Great Britain. Air-cooled, single trans-verse cylinder. 89 × 102 mm., 631 cc. Side valves. High-tension magneto ignition. Two forward speeds, epi-cyclic gears. Chain drive. Half-elliptic front springs, quarter-elliptic rear springs.

VALVELESS 25 H.P.

56

Valveless 25 h.p. 1910. Great Britain. Water-cooled, two vertical cylinders in line. 133 × 140 mm., 3892 cc. (× 2). Two-stroke. High-tension magneto ignition. Three forward speeds. Shaft drive. Half-elliptic springs front and rear.

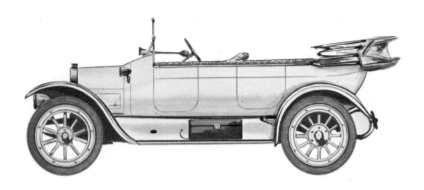

57

Brush 10 h.p. 1910. U.S.A. Water-cooled, single vertical cylinder. 102 × 127 mm., 1029 cc. Side valves. Coil and battery ignition. Two forward speeds, epicyclic gears. Chain final drive. Coil-spring suspension front and rear.

BENZ 20/35 H.P.

58

Benz 20/35 h.p. 1910, 1911. Germany. Water-cooled, four vertical cylinders in line. 105 × 140 mm., 4851 cc. Side valves. High-tension magneto and coil ignition. Four forward speeds. Shaft drive. Half-elliptic springs front and rear.

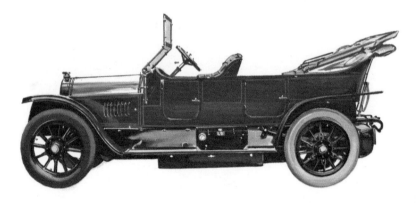

ADLER 7/15 PS

59

Adler 7/15 PS. 1910. Germany. Water-cooled, four vertical cylinders in line. 75 × 100 mm., 1768 cc. Side valves. High-tension magneto and coil ignition. Three forward speeds. Shaft drive. Half-elliptic springs front and rear.

60

Stoewer Typ B6, 1910, Typ C1, 1913. Germany. Water-cooled, four vertical cylinders in line. *Top:* 78 × 118 mm., 2025 cc.; *bottom:* 75 × 88 mm., 1546 cc. Side valves. High-tension magneto ignition. Four forward speeds. Shaft drive. *Top:* half-elliptic springs front and rear; *bottom:* half-elliptic front springs, three-quarter elliptic rear springs.

61

Phänomobil 4/6 PS. 1910. Germany. Air-cooled, two cylinders in vee formation. 82 x 84 mm., 880 cc. Side valves. High-tension magneto and coil
ignition. Two forward speeds. Epicyclic gears. Chain drive. Front suspension by
coil spring, rear cee springs.

BIANCHI 20/30 H.P., 14/20 H.P.

62

Bianchi 20/30 h.p., 14/20 h.p. 1910. Italy. Water-cooled, four vertical cylinders in line. *Top:* 110 × 130 mm., 4939 cc.; *bottom:* 90 × 115 mm., 2920 cc. Side valves. High-tension magneto ignition. Four forward speeds. Shaft drive. Half-elliptic springs front and rear.

63

Métallurgique 12 CV. 1910, 1911. Belgium. Water-cooled, four vertical cylinders in line. 80 ×130 mm., 2615 cc. Side valves. High-tension magneto ignition. Four forward speeds. Shaft drive. Front half-elliptic springs, rear cantilever springs.

LE ZÈBRE 4 CV

64

Le Zèbre 4 CV. 1911. France. Water-cooled, single cylinder. 85 × 106 mm., 600 cc. Side valves. High-tension magneto ignition. Two forward speeds. Shaft drive. Half-elliptic springs front and rear.

65

Turcat-Méry 18 CV. 1911. France. Water-cooled, four vertical cylinders in line. 90 × 130 mm., 3307 cc. Side valves. High-tension magneto ignition. Four forward speeds. Shaft drive. Half-elliptic springs front and rear.

CLÉMENT-BAYARD TYPE 4M

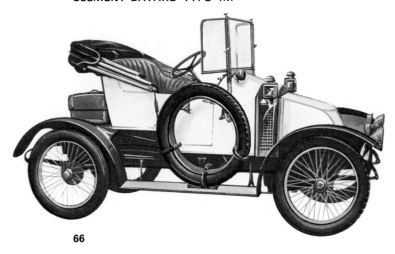

66

Clément-Bayard Type 4M. 1911, 1912. France. Water-cooled, four vertical cylinders in line. 60 ×120 mm., 1354 cc. Side valves. High-tension magneto ignition. Three forward speeds. Shaft drive.

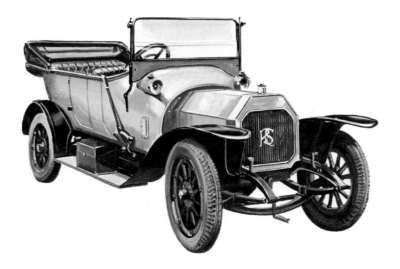

67

Rochet-Schneider 25 CV. 1911. France. Water-cooled, four vertical cylinders in line. 105 × 140 mm., 4851 cc. Side valves. High-tension magneto ignition. Four forward speeds. Shaft drive. Front half-elliptic springs, rear three-quarter-elliptic springs.

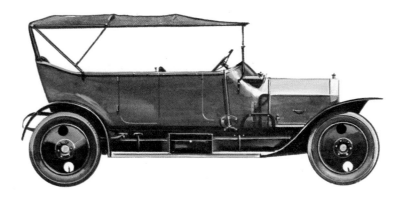

WOLSELEY 16/20 H.P.

68

Wolseley 16/20 h.p. 1911, 1912. Great Britain. Water-cooled, four vertical cylinders in line. 90 ×121 mm., 3080 cc. Side valves. High-tension magneto ignition. Four forward speeds. Shaft drive. Half-elliptic front springs, three-quarter-elliptic rear springs.

69

Austin 15 h.p. 1911. Great Britain. Water-cooled, four vertical cylinders in line. 89 ×114 mm., 2840 cc. Side valves. High-tension magneto and coil and battery ignition. Four forward speeds. Shaft drive. Front half-elliptic springs, rear full-elliptic springs.

JOWETT

70

Jowett. 1911 (?). Great Britain. Water-cooled, two horizontal cylinders. 72 × 102 mm., 826 cc. Side valves. High-tension magneto ignition. Three forward speeds. Shaft drive. Half-elliptic springs front and rear. Tiller steering.

71

Arrol-Johnston 15·9 h.p. 1911. Great Britain. Water-cooled, four vertical cylinders in line. 80 ×120 mm., 2414 cc. Side valves. High-tension magneto ignition. Four forward speeds. Shaft drive. Half-elliptic springs at front, full-elliptic springs at rear.

72

American Underslung 50 h.p. 1911. U.S.A.
Water-cooled, four vertical cylinders in line.
136·5 × 140 mm., 8165 cc. Side valves.
High-tension magneto and coil ignition.
Four forward speeds. Shaft drive. Half-elliptic
springs front and rear.

73

Franklin Model D. 1911. U.S.A. Air-cooled, six vertical cylinders in line. 102 × 102 mm., 5000 cc. Pushrod-operated overhead valves. High-tension magneto ignition. Three forward speeds. Shaft drive. Full-elliptic suspension front and rear.

BUICK 24/30 H.P., BEDFORD-BUICK 15/18 H.P.

74

Buick 24/30 h.p., Bedford-Buick 15/18 h.p. 1911. U.S.A. Water-cooled, four vertical cylinders in line. *Top:* 108 ×114 mm., 4537 cc.; *bottom:* 95 ×95 mm., 2694 cc. Pushrod-operated overhead valves. High-tension magneto and coil ignition. Two forward speeds. Epicyclic gearing. Shaft drive. Front half-elliptic springs, rear full-elliptic springs.

CHEVROLET MODEL C, CLASSIC SIX

Chevrolet Model C, 1911, Classic Six, 1912. U.S.A. Water-cooled, six vertical cylinders in line. 90 × 127 mm., 4850 cc. Side valves. High-tension magneto ignition. Three forward speeds. Shaft drive. Half-elliptic springs front and rear, auxiliary transverse spring at rear.

STANLEY 10 H.P.

76

Stanley 10 h.p. 1911. U.S.A. Steam engine, simple, double-acting. Two horizontal cylinders. Vertical multi-tube boiler, kerosene burner. Full-elliptic springs front and rear.

77

Opel 6/16 PS. 1911. Germany. Water-cooled, four vertical cylinders in line. 70 × 100 mm., 1540 cc. Side valves. High-tension magneto ignition. Four forward speeds. Shaft drive. Half-elliptic springs front and rear.

GRÄF UND STIFT 18/32 PS

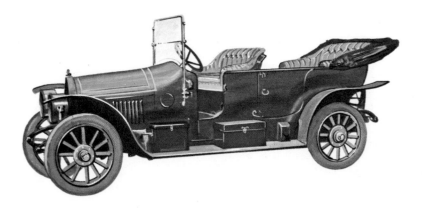

78

Gräf und Stift 18/32 PS. 1911. Austria. Water-cooled, four vertical cylinders in line. 115 × 140 mm., 5880 cc. Side valves. High-tension magneto and coil ignition. Four forward speeds. Shaft drive. Front half-elliptic springs, rear three-quarter-elliptic springs.

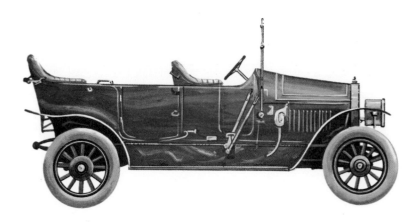

79

FN Type 1560, Type 1600. 1911. Belgium. Water-cooled, four vertical cylinders in line. 74 × 90 mm., 1545 cc. Side valves. High-tension magneto ignition. *Top:* three forward speeds; *bottom:* four forward speeds. Shaft drive. Half-elliptic springs front and rear.

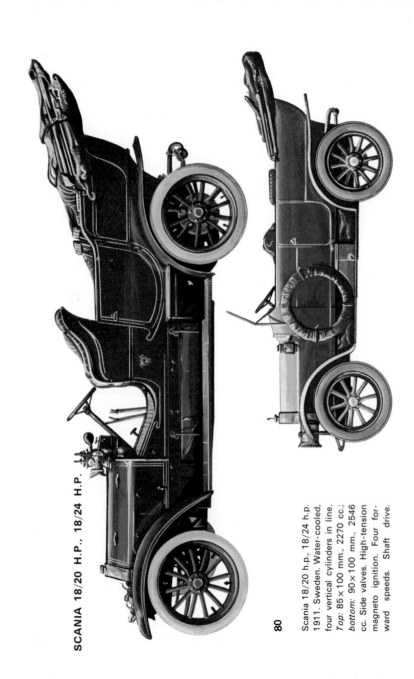

SCANIA 18/20 H.P., 18/24 H.P.

80

Scania 18/20 h.p., 18/24 h.p. 1911. Sweden. Water-cooled, four vertical cylinders in line. *Top:* 85×100 mm., 2270 cc.; *bottom:* 90×100 mm., 2546 cc. Side valves. High-tension magneto ignition. Four forward speeds. Shaft drive.

81

Berliet 12 CV. 1912. France. Water-cooled, four vertical cylinders in line. 80×120 mm., 2408 cc. Side valves. High-tension magneto ignition. Four forward speeds. Shaft drive. Half-elliptic front springs, three-quarter-elliptic rear springs.

PANHARD-LEVASSOR 15 CV

82

Panhard-Levassor 15 CV. 1912. France. Water-cooled, four vertical cylinders in line. 80×130 mm., 2614 cc. Double sleeve valves. High-tension magneto ignition. Four forward speeds. Shaft drive. Half-elliptic springs front and rear.

83

H.L. 10/15 CV, 12/18 CV. 1912. France. Water-cooled, four vertical cylinders
in line. *Top:* 76 × 130 mm., 2360 cc.; *bottom:* 80 × 150 mm., 3000 cc. Side
valves. High-tension magneto ignition. Two forward speeds. Shaft drive.
Independent front suspension by sliding pillars and coil springs, half-elliptic
rear springs.

SCHNEIDER TH. 18 CV

84

Schneider Th. 18 CV. 1912. France. Water-cooled, four vertical cylinders in line. 95 × 130 mm., 3680 cc. Side valves. High-tension magneto ignition. Four forward speeds. Shaft drive.

85

Belsize 10/12 h.p. 1912. Great Britain. Water-cooled, four vertical cylinders in line. 69×130 mm., 1945 cc. Side valves. High-tension magneto ignition. Three forward speeds. Shaft drive. Half-elliptic springs front and rear.

ROVER TWELVE

86

Rover Twelve. 1912. Great Britain. Water-cooled, four vertical cylinders in line. 75 × 130 mm., 2297 cc. Side valves. High-tension magneto ignition. Four forward speeds. Shaft drive. Half-elliptic springs front and rear.

87

Iris 15 h.p. 1912. Great Britain. Water-cooled, four vertical cylinders in line. 80 × 114 mm., 2293 cc. Side valves. High-tension magneto ignition. Three forward speeds. Shaft drive. Half-elliptic springs front and rear.

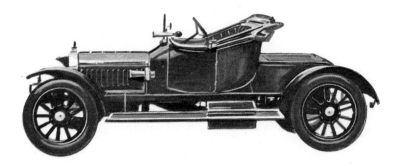

88

Sunbeam 12/16 h.p. 1912. Great Britain. Water-cooled, four vertical cylinders in line. 80×150 mm., 3010 cc. Side valves. High-tension magneto ignition. Four forward speeds. Shaft drive. Half-elliptic front springs, three-quarter-elliptic rear springs.

89

Morris-Oxford. 1913. Great Britain. Water-cooled, four vertical cylinders in line. 60 × 90 mm., 1018 cc. High-tension magneto ignition. Three forward speeds. Shaft drive. Half-elliptic front springs, three-quarter-elliptic rear springs.

K.R.I.T. 25/30 H.P.

90

K.R.I.T. 25/30 h.p. 1912. U.S.A. Water-cooled, four vertical cylinders in line. 95 × 102 mm., 2898 cc. Side valves. High-tension magneto ignition. Three forward speeds. Shaft drive. Half-elliptic front springs, full-elliptic rear springs.

91

Rambler 38 h.p. 1912. U.S.A. Water-cooled, four vertical cylinders in line. 114 × 114 mm., 4700 cc. Side valves. High-tension magneto ignition. Three forward speeds. Shaft drive. Half-elliptic front springs, three-quarter-elliptic rear springs.

REX-SIMPLEX TYP C

92

Rex-Simplex Typ C. 1913, 1912. Germany. Water-cooled, four vertical cylinders in line. 100 × 140 mm., 4500 cc. Side valves. High-tension magneto ignition. Four forward speeds. Shaft drive. Half-elliptic front springs, three-quarter-elliptic rear springs.

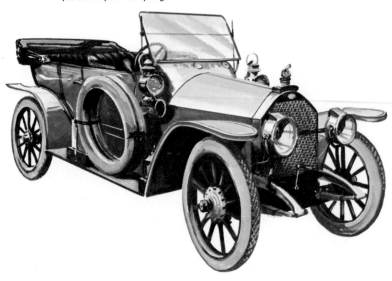

93

Fiat Tipo 51 Zero. 1912. Italy. Water-cooled, four vertical cylinders in line. 70×120 mm., 1847 cc. Side valves. High-tension magneto ignition. Four forward speeds. Shaft drive. Half-elliptic front springs, three-quarter-elliptic rear springs.

MINERVA 16 H.P.

94

Minerva 16 h.p. 1912. Belgium. Water-cooled, four vertical cylinders in line. 80 × 125 mm., 2514 cc. Sleeve valves. High-tension magneto and coil ignition. Four forward speeds. Shaft drive. Half-elliptic front springs, three-quarter-elliptic rear springs.

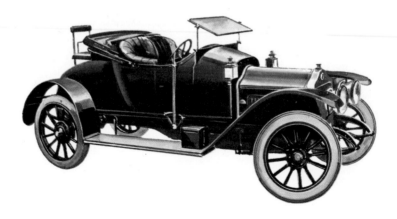

95

Spyker. 1912. Holland. Water-cooled, two cylinders. 80 × 108 mm., 1100 cc.
Two transverse camshafts. High-tension magneto ignition. Two forward speeds.
Shaft drive. Half-elliptic springs front and rear.

96

Stella 20/30 CV. 1912. Switzerland. Water-cooled, four vertical cylinders in line. 90×160 mm., 4073 cc. Side valves. High-tension magneto ignition. Four forward speeds. Shaft drive. Half-elliptic springs front and rear.

1 MORS TYPE R, 1905, France

Emile Mors ran an old-established firm of Parisian electrical engineers which in 1896 built its first car. This was a Benz-like machine with slow-turning single-cylinder engine and belt drive; but late in the same year a completely original design appeared that reflected Mors's interest in electrical matters. It employed low-tension ignition from a battery and dynamo, this being the first successful application of the dynamo to the motor vehicle. These were the Mors's most important features; it also had an engine with four cylinders in vee formation, but this was not continued after 1899, being replaced by a horizontally opposed twin. Nor was the dynamo, in this application, though it became universal with the coming of electric lighting and starting much later. Henri Brasier was chief engineer from 1899 until 1902, when he joined Georges Richard. Under him, the Mors developed into a completely conventional, well-made, generally large and fast car that was for several years the only serious rival to Panhard-Levassor in major races, winning the Paris–Berlin event of 1901 and leading the Paris–Madrid Race of 1903 when it was stopped at Bordeaux. Brasier was responsible for these machines and their touring relations, which had low-tension magneto ignition as early as 1899. An in-line four-cylinder chain-driven 10-h.p. machine on Panhard lines was introduced in 1901 that set the Mors trend for biggish, powerful cars. In 1902, they were among the first

French car manufacturers to go over to the *système* Mercedes, and from then until 1907, pair-cast cylinders, side valves in a T head, mechanically-operated inlet valves, chain drive, steel frames, honeycomb radiators and gate change were the order of the day. There were five models in 1905, all basically similar, of which the Type R 16/18 CV is illustrated. It had a 2·4-litre engine, the low-tension ignition used until 1906, and four forward speeds.

2 COTTEREAU 14 CV, 1904, 18 CV, 1905, France

Cottereau et Cie of Dijon made bicycles and motor-cycles, and also—from 1898 to 1911—cars (most of them of original concept). Initially, Louis and Henri Cottereau specialized in the vee engine. The first of the line, a vee-twin, was otherwise a conventional enough *voiturette* of the turn of the century, with its air-cooling, coil ignition, tubular frame and chain drive. A 1·4-litre version took part in the Paris–Toulouse Race of 1900, and vee-fours were entered in the Paris–Bordeaux event of the following year. The latter's engines had water-cooled cylinder-heads. Vee-fours raced in 1901 and 1902, in the Paris–Berlin and Paris–Vienna Races. They finished on both occasions. By late 1903, the one original model had been supplemented by several more. As well as a 7-h.p. and 10-h.p. twin, there was a 5-h.p. single, and at the other end of the range a catalogued 16-h.p. vee-four. All cars were chain-driven and had three forward speeds, while the biggest boasted the very modern feature of high-tension magneto ignition. A further departure came in 1904, with a three-cylinder in-line type of orthodox Mercedes type (side valves in a T-head arrangement, honeycomb radiator). The three-cylinder was continued as late as 1908, with modifications. The cars illustrated are earlier versions. The manufacturing company was unusual, for a small concern, in that it made its own engines, gear-boxes, and carburettors instead of buying out.

3 MASS 8 CV, 1905, France

At one time when the Mass car was sold in Britain, it appeared under the slogan 'Simple — Silent — Successful'. Simple the model shown here may have been, since it used an 8-h.p. single-cylinder De Dion engine; silent it probably was not, for the same reason; and successful it never was, either in Britain or in its country of origin, France. The Mass seems to have been one of the many vehicles different in name but uniformly indifferent in quality that were all made by the firm of Lacoste & Battmann of Levallois; though the address of the selling organization, Automobiles Mass, was another Paris suburb, Courbevoie. The car emerged from there from 1903 onwards; from 1912, another make, Pierron, thought by some to be merely the Mass under another name, was sold from the same address. The cars sold in our period were all conventional. The first, the 6 h.p. of 1903, was powered by De Dion; in the same year an Aster-engined 4½ h.p. was offered. The latter had a tubular frame (like the De Dion

it wasn't), but the 8 h.p. had a channel-section frame, a three-speed gear-box, and shaft drive to a conventional back axle—apart from the engine, there was little De Dion about it. The Mass survived into the early 1920s, still as a very sedate and conservative piece of machinery. Not only were the origins of the Mass confusing; the make's wide range of models has the same effect upon historians. The cause of the diversity is quite simple: the Mass was always an assembled car with no particular character at all, its specifications depending on the fluctuating availability and price of its components. It is included here as a representative of its nondescript if numerous breed.

4 VAUXHALL 9 h.p., 1905, Great Britain

The Vauxhall Ironworks of Lambeth, in London, started their motor manufacturing career with single-cylinder cars, the 5 h.p. of 1903 and its successor the 6 h.p. of 1904. Both were fairly primitive *voiturettes*, buyers of the 5 h.p. paying for their cheapness with the lack of such refinements as a reverse gear and a steering wheel (it had a tiller). Most of the 6-h.p. cars had both these features, but retained the chain drive of both models. So did the next type, the altogether bigger and heavier (12 cwt.) three-cylinder machine first introduced late in 1904. Production (such as it was—only twenty cars were made) settled down in 1905, when two models were offered: a 12/14 h.p. which was soon dropped, and the car illustrated, the 9 h.p., of 80 × 110 mm.

bore and stroke and 1675 c.c. This engine was a T-head side-valve affair, with trembler coil ignition as before, but vertical cylinders, mechanically-operated inlet valves, and three forward speeds in a sliding-pinion gear-box and double chain drive instead of the single-cylinder car's two epicyclic speeds and single chain. Conventional half-elliptic springs replaced the earlier coil springs. The car was taken out of production in 1906, as the company's new four-cylinder cars (46) gained popularity.

5 DAIMLER 30 h.p., 1906, 35 h.p., 1905, Great Britain

From 1897, the Daimler Motor Company of Coventry, who in 1896 had acquired the British rights in the Daimler Motoren Gesellschaft's patents, started to make cars initially based on their German parents. From the start they acquired a reputation for strength, long life, and conservatism. By the end of 1901, with the appearance of the American Percy Martin as works manager, and the arrival of a new 22-h.p. car, the German Daimler influence had gone, but to the British car's accepted qualities was now added a quite considerable performance. After reorganization of the company in 1904, three cars were introduced that formed the basis for all Daimler models until the coming of the Knight double sleeve-valve engine in 1908, and a worm-drive rear axle in 1910. The 28/36 h.p. that was the biggest of the new models introduced the famous ribbed radiator in cast aluminium. They were chain-driven, with four forward speeds and a dead axle, and retained a conventional

T-head valve layout and pair-cast cylinders, with (at long last) mechanically-operated inlet valves. There was an option of coil or magneto ignition. The largest model was the 10·6 litre 45 h.p. of 1906–7. The cars shown are a 1906 30 h.p. (top), and a 1905 35 h.p. Both were four-cylinder machines. The former, like all Daimlers of its generation, was utterly reliable, even at the speeds of 50 m.p.h. and more which its 7·2-litre engine permitted when a reasonably light body was fitted. Indeed, in these years Daimlers went in for competitions in a very big way, annexing more awards in British speed events than any other make. They competed energetically in foreign contests such as the 1906 Coppa d'Oro, the Kaiserpreis and Targa Florio races of 1907, the Herkomer and Prince Henry tours, and American events. The Italian races saw Coventry-built Daimlers competing under the name by which they were sold in Italy; De Luca Daimler. This Naples concern made Daimlers under licence from 1906 to 1908.

6 ROLLS-ROYCE 15 h.p., 1905, Great Britain

In his search for the ultimate in refinement, silence, and flexibility, Henry Royce of Royce Ltd., starting in 1904, made one of the finest two-cylinder cars on the market in these respects. His agreement with the Hon. C. S. Rolls, whose firm C. S. Rolls & Company were to sell his output, stipulated a wide range of models, and 1905 saw not only the twin, but also the four-cylinder 20 h.p.—the most popular model by then—a 30-h.p. six of which very few were made, and half a dozen of the 15 h.p. three-cylinder car shown. The complication of the range was to be offset by interchangeability of parts, but although the three-litre 15-h.p. engine shared the overhead-inlet valve layout and the cylinder dimensions of the rest, its cylinders were cast separately. Not until the advent of the famous Silver Ghost (17) were Royce's engines cast in threes; the others were pair-cast, including the 30 h.p. There were three forward speeds. The 15 h.p. went as every Rolls-Royce went: beautifully. It was of significance only as an interim type, built at a time when Royce was looking for his ideal (which he found in the Silver Ghost), and when Rolls still considered, as was normal thinking, that a motor manufacturer must carry several models in order to reach as many markets as possible.

7 CRAIG-DORWALD S-TYPE, 1905, Great Britain

One of the obscurer products of London's motor industry, made from 1903 to 1912, was the Craig-Dorwald. In common with Frederick Simms's Daimler Motor Syndicate a dozen years earlier, its makers were first known for marine engines emanating from the suburb of Putney. But they (first called the Putney Motor Company and then the Ailsa-Craig Motor Company) also made a few road vehicles. At first commercial and public service needs were catered for; a vee-twelve engine developing 150 b.h.p. was developed in 1904, and a tractor for

buses and heavy delivery at around the same time. The normal Craig-Dorwald car was a twin, but that shown was the S-Type four-cylinder, a big, more luxurious machine. Its engine developed 36 b.h.p., which was very little from over seven litres. This unit was twice the basic Ailsa-Craig engine, which was a two-cylinder of 18 b.h.p. also called the S-Type, used (like the other types) for marine work as well, and turning at a conservative 950 r.p.m. A single-cylinder car was offered, that was half of it. The immense 21-litre twelve-cylinder unit was simply six times the basic twin. Quite different, and just as advanced for its day, was the single overhead-camshaft single-cylinder engine made in 1904, but not fitted to a car.

8 PIERCE GREAT ARROW 28 h.p., 1905, U.S.A.

The first car offered by the George N. Pierce Company of Buffalo (makers of various other hardware, including bird-cages, ice-boxes, and bicycles) was a close copy of the French 2¾-h.p. single-cylinder De Dion Bouton, called the Pierce Motorette, that saw the light in 1901. It was not unusual in being a foreign design (nor in having an un-sprung back axle), but in that its deviser, David Fergusson, plumped for a small, high-revving engine instead of the large, lazy unit normal in America at the time. The little car grew up by stages, into the 8-h.p. Stanhope of 1903, but in the same year a conventional bigger car appeared, the earliest Pierce Arrow, with two-cylinder engine at the front, cone clutch, sliding-pinion gear-box, and shaft drive to a sprung bevel-gear axle. The first machines of the type illustrated, the Great Arrows, came in 1904. These were powerful cars with four-cylinder engines with mechanically-operated inlet valves in a T-head arrangement and separately-cast cylinders, at first of 24 h.p., and then, in 1905–6, of 28 h.p. and 40 h.p. A 28 h.p. is illustrated; the car on which Percy P. Pierce, son of George N., tied for first place in the 1905 Glidden Tour. Its 4·4-litre engine could turn at up to 1,600 r.p.m., and dual ignition by high-tension magneto and coil was provided. Fergusson's designs were fast, expensive cars of very high quality, that became one of the leading luxury makes in the United States. Success not only in the 1905 Glidden Tour but also in the 1906, 1907, 1908, and 1909 events brought it immediate fame. A six-cylinder car, the layout on which the firm was to concentrate, came in 1907, but the big fours were continued until 1909.

9 PEERLESS 35 h.p., 1905, 24 h.p., 1904, U.S.A.

The Peerless Motor Car Company of Cleveland, Ohio, which began to make cars in 1900, grew out of a bicycle manufacturer, which was normal enough, but the latter originated as a maker of clothes-wringers, which was original. When, at the other end of the Car Company's career, in 1931, it became the Peerless Corporation, the factory was converted into a brewery. In between, it produced some of the finest luxury-class cars seen in the

United States. However, like the Pierce (8), a machine of comparable status in the coming years, the Peerless started humbly enough, as a De Dion-type single-cylinder *voiturette*. Similar vehicles followed during 1901, but in that year Louis Mooers arrived as chief engineer. While the 1902 cars had two-cylinder power units, they were otherwise firmly designed on big-car lines, with front engines, mechanically-operated inlet valves, sliding-pinion gear-boxes, and shaft drive. The 1903 cars settled into the familiar Mercedes pattern (apart from the shaft drive), with their four-cylinder T-head engines in 24-h.p. and 35-h.p. form and honeycomb radiators. The 1904 24 h.p. illustrated above had an 'over-square' engine. The upper illustration shows a 35 h.p., which in 1905 cost $4,000 (£800 then), a great deal to pay for a car in America.

10 MERCEDES 35/40 PS, 1906, 1905, Germany

By the time the cars shown in the illustration were built, in 1905 and 1906, the Daimler Motoren Gesellschaft was (justifiably) resting on its technical laurels. The 35-h.p. Mercedes of 1901, the first Daimler-made car to bear this type name, had set the international standard for luxury machines. Wilhelm Maybach had set out to design a really fast car that was also safe and pleasant to drive (a hitherto unknown combination), and what resulted was so good a general-purpose vehicle that it became the prototype of the modern motor-car in shape, and to some extent in running and handling qualities. It combined for the first time a powerful, flexible engine of the most modern design (with mechanically-operated inlet valves and low-tension magneto ignition) with a low centre of gravity, a pressed-steel frame, a gate-type gear-change (instead of the common progressive type), and an efficient honeycomb radiator directly in front of the engine. The result was so effective that, by 1904, every important maker of high-priced cars the world over had copied the Mercedes pattern. Competition successes, particularly a win in the 1903 Gordon Bennett Race, heightened the appeal of the name. The 35/40-h.p. model shown differed little from its original; there was no need for change yet. It was conventional, but it had made the convention. It had four paircast cylinders totalling 5·3 litres, with side valves in a T head. Neither high-tension magnetos nor shaft drive were seen on any Mercedes before 1907–8.

11 NAG 20/24 PS, 1906, 1905, Germany

The Neue Automobilgesellschaft was best known for its small cars in the pre-1914 era, from the first NAG of all (the 5 PS *voiturette* of 1900 with unit-built engine, gear-box, and final-drive assembly); but by late 1904 there was a big Mercedes-type bi-bloc four in the range, with 5·2 litres, chain drive, and four speeds. This Typ B, like its twin-cylinder stablemate, was designed by Joseph Vollmer, formerly of the Bergmann's Industriewerk of Gaggenau (35).

The side valves were arranged in T-head formation, and the model rating was 20/24 PS. The indicated 24 b.h.p. was developed at 1,000 r.p.m. Maximum speed was around 40 m.p.h. 1906 and 1905 examples of the model are shown. It was joined in 1905 by the bigger Typ B2.

12 RENAULT 20/30 CV, 1906, France

Renault had initially made his name with excellent and popular little *voiturettes* that had pioneered the combination in one motor-car of shaft drive to a sprung live axle. Seen in conjunction with a front engine driving through a friction clutch and a three-speed gear-box with direct drive on top, it is clear (in retrospect) that the layout of the modern car had arrived. From 1899, other makes began to copy it. Having made his mark, Louis Renault was content to rest on his laurels, in the technological sense. His car grew up in the normal way—water-cooling instead of air-cooling in 1900; wheel steering in 1901; his own engines (instead of De Dion or Aster bought out) from 1903; two- and four-cylinder units supplementing the single in the same year, with mechanically-operated inlet valves on the four. The Renault of 1903 onwards was unconventional in only two ways: the original tumbler-action gear-box with quadrant change persisted as late as 1914, and the radiator had retired behind the engine, leaving the much-copied 'coal-scuttle' hood. The Renault was popular because all types were relatively flexible, smooth, and quiet, and well-made, reliable, and long-lasting by any standards. It was by a long way the best-liked middle-class car in France, and made a deep impression in the same market in whatever country it penetrated. The biggest of the range in 1906, which had then been current for two years and was to stay in the catalogue for another four, was the car shown. The 4·4-litre 20/30 CV engine, developing its 30 b.h.p. at 1,000 r.p.m., could propel even formal bodywork like that illustrated at 50 m.p.h.; though the normal cruising gait would be about 40 m.p.h. in deference to windage and a high centre of gravity.

13 **ALBION A6,** 1906, 1910, Great Britain

The Albion Motor Car Company of Glasgow, like Arrol-Johnston (71), made cars of solid and hard-wearing character, suited to the poor roads and lack of repair and service facilities in Scotland in the early years of the century. Since its founders, T. Blackwood Murray and N. O. Fulton, had been among the originators of the Arrol-Johnston as well, it is not surprising that the A1 and A2 Albions shared the early eccentricities of the latter, including a slow-turning horizontal twin-cylinder engine centrally-mounted and driving to the rear wheels by single chain, low-tension flywheel magneto ignition, and a horse-carriage type of coachwork retrograde even in 1901. The A2 was basically similar and both were made until 1903. The 12-h.p. A3 of that year and the bigger 16 h.p. that followed

had a vertical engine at the front and double side-chain drive; these twins, which did not differ fundamentally from the first, were offered until 1914 as passenger and commercial vehicles. However, Albion, like Arrol-Johnston a year later, found the pressure to 'go conventional' in the passenger car field irresistible, and the four-cylinder T-head 24-h.p. A6 of 1906, illustrated here in 1906 and 1910 form, was the outcome. This was intended as a luxury car, and had four forward speeds. It retained chain drive, a dead axle, and low-tension magneto ignition, by now an old-fashioned feature. Engine speed was conservative, too, at 1,200 r.p.m. It and the A3 were very popular, necessitating factory expansion; 221 chassis were built in 1906, made by 283 employees. The A6 was the only chassis made for passenger cars alone, and no new chassis intended even partly for such use came until the 15-h.p. A 14 of 1911, which was also the firm's first shaft-drive, live-axle product. It had worm final drive. The expensive 24 h.p. had gone out of production in 1910.

14 **COMPOUND 12/15 h.p.,** 1906, U.S.A.

The Eisenhuth Horseless Vehicle Company of Middletown, Connecticut, did itself an injustice in its name, with its connotations of primitive simplicity, for its product, the Compound car, was anything but either of these things. Made from 1903 to 1907, it was designed by John Unser and powered by a Graham-Fox engine, remarkable for the fact that it had two high-pressure four-stroke cylinders and one low-pressure two-stroke cylinder, which energized not only the driving wheels but also the compressed-air brakes. A 16 h.p. or Model 5 of 1906 is shown. A 24/28 h.p. was also offered. The single two-stroke cylinder ran on the pressure of the exhaust gases from the other two cylinders on either side of it. Exceptional smoothness and silence were claimed for the design, of which a six-cylinder version appeared in 1907.

15 PICCOLO 5 PS, 1906, Germany

In 1904 H. Ruppe & Sohn of Apolda in Thuringia, having built motor-cycles from 1902, began to make the *voiturette* illustrated; it had a vee-twin fan-cooled engine of 75 × 80 mm., giving 704 c.c. The inlet valves were automatic, there was coil ignition, and transmission was on 'large-car' lines, with a cone clutch, two-speed sliding-pinion gear-box in unit with the engine, and shaft drive to a live axle. Rated at 5 PS, it was made until 1907. The indicated b.h.p. was developed at 1,300 r.p.m., but the little engine was capable of 2,000 r.p.m.; a high speed for the time. Maximum speed was around 30 m.p.h. This excellent and popular machine of very interesting design was developed progressively into the 7 PS of 1907–10, now with mechanically-operated overhead inlet valves and a longer stroke, and three forward speeds. The engine was further enlarged in the Piccolo-Apollo Typ A of 1910–12, though the basic design remained the same.

16 DE DION BOUTON TYPE AV, 1908, 1907, France

From the viewpoint of the popularization of the automobile in Europe, the name of De Dion Bouton can be said to have had a greater influence than any other, since it was borne by the first truly practical small car. This was the single-cylinder machine, current from the beginning (in 1899) to 1912 in various forms. The engine was strong and reliable, yet extremely efficient, being high-revving. The little car was not only quite fast but easy to control, too; another feature which set it aside from most of its contemporaries of the same type. So did its unconventional drive. The final drive and differential assembly was mounted on the chassis, and drive thence was by shafts independent of the rear axle, which carried only the wheels. Unsprung weight was reduced, but the object of the design was to allow the rear axle to move in relation to the chassis without using chain drive. De Dion-type drive was revived after the Second World War on some of the most sophisticated high-performance cars, with the first purpose in mind. 'Modernization' took place late in 1905, when the *voiturette* began to grow up. Two four-cylinder cars were already listed. The original tubular chassis started to give way to a pressed-steel frame; the radiator (now with vertical tubes) was raised from the underslung to a front-of-engine position on twins and fours in 1906; the constant-mesh two- and three-speed expanding-clutch gear-boxes gave way to the conventional three-speed sliding-pinion affair; and mechanically-operated inlet valves came in 1907. In fact, growing-up meant becoming conventional, in all respects other than final drive, which survived in its original form until 1911. The single remained popular until the demise of the 8 h.p. in 1909, but from late 1902 there had been a 12-h.p. two-cylinder car in the catalogue. From the start, this had three forward speeds, and pressure lubrication of the engine. The 1908 (top) and 1907 (bottom) Type AV 10-h.p. twin shown had all the 'improvements' noted in addition, and though much less famous than the single, was just as well made and as sound a car. It proved itself in this respect when two examples finished the gruelling Peking–Paris Trial of 1907. Its engine, rated at 10 h.p. and with a bore and stroke of 80 × 120 mm., giving 1,204 c.c., could propel the 15-cwt. two-passenger car at between 30 and 35 m.p.h. This was about the same as the single's maximum, but the latter was lighter.

17 ROLLS-ROYCE
40/50 h.p., 1907,
Great Britain

Because his engineering standards were so high in an age when the average car was a rough and noisy beast, Henry Royce was preoccupied with the achievement of silence and smoothness, as can be seen even in his first machine, the Royce of 1904. What was basically a Decauville, a worthy French import of no great distinction, was turned into one of the quietest and silkiest two-cylinder machines on the market partly by redesign, but mainly by extremely careful workmanship. When the Hon. C. S. Rolls took over the selling of the car, its name was changed to Rolls-Royce. In the same year of 1904, the now-familiar radiator shape arrived. Four- and six-cylinder engines were on show at the Paris Salon in the very same year, for the ultimate in smoothness and flexibility could not be achieved with a twin. The last-named was offered into 1906, but by 1905 it had been supplemented by a short-lived three-cylinder machine (6), the four-cylinder Twenty, and by the firm's first six, the Thirty, a true luxury car. In 1906, however, Royce designed a bigger six-cylinder engine, with side valves in an L-head instead of overhead inlet valves. The cylinders, cast in threes in place of the more usual pairs, had a total capacity of 7,036 c.c., from which a modest 48 b.h.p. at 1,200 r.p.m. was forthcoming. The chassis was much the same as that of the 30 h.p. and 20 h.p. The first complete 40/50-h.p. Rolls-Royce was shown at the 1906 Olympia Show. Such was the partners' faith in it that their conventional multimodel policy was dropped in 1907: from now on, all their eggs were in the one basket. The thirteenth car built was christened 'Silver Ghost', and the name stuck to the model. The stroke was lengthened from 114 mm. to 121 mm. in 1909 to obtain more performance, now providing 7,428 c.c. and 50 b.h.p. The immediate aim of a larger engine had been to compete effectively in the Two Thousand Miles Trial of the previous year, in which the make was the second most successful car after the Vauxhall, but in the longer view the firm had an eye on the faster 60-h.p. Napier, the Rolls' main competitor. A four-speed gear-box was fitted from 1906 to 1909, as on earlier models, but the geared-up top was noisy as well as unnecessary, so from 1909 until 1913 only three forward speeds were provided. In normal town and touring use no more was needed, since the engine was so flexible. Three to 65 m.p.h. was possible on top gear, in spite of the normal final-drive ratio of 2·9:1. This was as well, since the only fault in the handling of a car otherwise superlatively easy to control lay in the difficult gear-change. Otherwise, by the standards of the time the steering and the clutch were light. Great smoothness was attained: the vibration period suffered by the 30 h.p. and other sixes with pair-cast cylinders was absent. It was not, of course, a completely silent car, but its engine was quieter than any other on the market: this included the United States, if the American Press reaction after the New York Show of 1907 was to be believed. Royce himself said that the 40/50 was the 'finest thing I have ever done'.

18 STANDARD 30 h.p., 1907, 40 h.p., 1910, Great Britain

Before he began serious car production, R. W. Maudslay of the Standard Motor Company built engines for other manufacturers, one- and two-cylinder prototype cars of advanced design for 1903, and three- and four-cylinder machines in penny packets during 1904 and 1905. At the end of 1905, that skilful salesman Gharles Friswell took over the sole agency for the make. However, the Standard cars that subsequently

appeared (in quantity for the first time) were, indeed, standard in specification; Friswell knew that the public disliked eccentricities as much as they appreciated solidity, reliability, and moderate price: all of which Maudslay gave them. The backbone of the new expanded policy was the 3·3-litre (later 4 litre) 20-h.p. six-cylinder car already in the range (the engine of which could be supplied separately to other makers). It had a three-speed gear-box. By spring 1906 there was a bigger 30 h.p. available (also a six), which had four forward speeds and five litres, and a 50 h.p. A 40 h.p. of 6·2 litres came in 1907; it had a bigger bore than the 30 h.p. There was also a 15 h.p. small six; Standard and Friswell had put their money on sixes, which was unusual at this date. An output of ten cars a week was planned. The 30 h.p. is illustrated in the form of a 1907 machine, while below it is a 40 h.p. of 1910. Their conservatism is apparent from the lack of change in their lines, but they were the most successful of the company's offerings until the coming of the 9·5-h.p. light car in 1913. The engines were T-head pair-cast units of modest output for their quite considerable size.

19 NEW EAGLE, 1907, 1908, Great Britain

The Eagle Engineering & Motor Company was formed in 1899 to make the Century Tandem, a motor tricar of a type common at the time and into the early 1900s, popular among motorists who wanted something one stage more comfortable than a motor bicycle. The concern's founder, Ralph Jackson, left in 1901 and began to make an almost identical vehicle under the name of Eagle. By 1903 he was building full-sized cars as well, with his own design of epicyclic gearing. Between then and 1907, everything from a single-passenger Runabout and a two-cylinder light car to the four-cylinder touring type shown was offered. The Eagle Engineering & Motor Company was wound up in that year, but Jackson continued to sell his cars through the St. George's Motor Car Company of Leeds, under the name of New Eagle. The upper illustration shows a 24/30-h.p. model. There was also a 35/45 h.p., while at the other end of the range was a 10/12 h.p., which utilized a four-cylinder Fafnir engine of German origin, with separately-cast cylinders.

20 **NAPIER 45 h.p.**, 1908,
    40 h.p., 1907,
    Great Britain

Late in 1903, D. Napier & Son had been responsible for offering to the public the world's earliest six-cylinder car to go into series production. From that time, S. F. Edge, who directed the company's sales and publicity, committed himself primarily to the six-cylinder luxury car, of which he was the leading enthusiast in Britain. When he had to make fours in order to fit the regulations of a race he wanted to enter, such as the 1908 Tourist Trophy, they bore another name—Hutton. In 1906 there were still two fours beside two sixes, all of them large, expensive cars, but from the following year the

models with fewer cylinders were definitely the poor relations: the 10-h.p. twin and 15-h.p. four-cylinder machines were often seen as taxis or in other commercial or public service use. Until the arrival of the Rolls-Royce Silver Ghost (17), Napier was Britain's premier make, thanks partly to Edge's promotion, and partly to the car's real merits of relative smoothness, flexibility, and hence comfort and ease of control. Its (L head, with pair-cast cylinders) engine was not quiet, and it suffered from the crankshaft vibration period common to most early sixes, but until the Rolls-Royce established itself, Napier led. By 1907–8, when the cars shown here were built, the Silver Ghost had arrived, but had not yet annexed the market. In view of Napier's hold on it, this could not happen overnight, especially as the Acton firm offered a variety of models at different prices. In fact its heyday came in the years 1909–11, when about 1,800 were built: more than 40 per cent of the company's entire passenger car output over the eighteen years 1906–24. 366 were made in 1909 and 801 in 1911. Perhaps not even the Silver Ghost could have accomplished Napier's decline alone: the departure of the dynamic Edge at the time it had become a serious rival took a lot of steam out of the company. The most popular model, if that is the word for a luxury car, was the 60-h.p. six, current from 1906 to 1910. It was certainly the most famous, for it had been used in Edge's most successful publicity *coup*, the 24 hours' run on Brooklands Motor Course in 1907, at an average speed of over 60 m.p.h. This year and the next, Napier racing cars (most of them stripped tourers) carried on the make's tradition of competition wins that had begun with its victory in the 1902 Gordon Bennett Race. The 40-h.p. T 20 and 45-h.p. T 23 sixes of 1907 and 1908 shown here were representative of the make at the peak of its fame, and were no mean performers themselves: in 1910, an open 45-h.p. tourer exceeded 66 m.p.h. at Brooklands.

21 THOMAS FLYER MODEL 6-70, 1907, U.S.A.

The E. R. Thomas Motor Car Company of Buffalo, makers of the car shown, grew out of the Buffalo Automobile and Auto-Bi Company, who made motor-cycles from 1899. Its cars were at first called simply Thomas, and were two-cylinder runabouts of conventional American type. In 1903 and 1904 a bigger three-cylinder car replaced the twins, and in its final form was a chain-driven machine on Mercedes lines (the fashionable guise for expensive cars). Then, in 1905, the three-cylinder car gave way to two big fours and an even bigger six, of 40, 50, and 60 h.p. respectively, still with double chain drive, called Thomas Flyers. This name was current until 1911, by which time all were sixes and had shaft drive. The Model 6-70, the development of the 60 h.p., was the best known on account of its victory in the New York–Paris Race of 1908, and was offered until 1912. The actual New York–Paris winner is illustrated here. Its 72-h.p. six-cylinder engine was of nearly 13 litres' capacity. The price in

normal touring form was $4,500 (£900) in 1907.

22 I.H.C., 1907, U.S.A.

The International Harvester Company, first of Chicago and later of Akron, Ohio, already with an established reputation for horse-drawn farm equipment, built experimental cars as early as 1901, but between 1906 and 1911 became the best-known of the manufacturers of those curious 'highwheelers' that were characteristic of the Middle West, and so suited to the hard work and terrible surfaces of those parts. They were really motorized buggies, applying the principles of the buggy — low weight, simplicity, strength, good carrying capacity, and exceptional ground clearance—to the motor-car. Most earlier I.H.C.s, like those of 1907 shown here, were powered by horizontally-opposed twin-cylinder fan-cooled engines, though water-cooled units (which still lived under the floorboards, not under the dummy hood of the later cars) could be specified. Both types had slow-turning engines of 14–16 h.p. and 3·2 litres, with mechanically-operated overhead valves, automatic lubrication and coil ignition. There was two-speed epicyclic transmission, and final drive by double side-chains. Tiller steering on the experimental models gave way to wheel. Like the horse-drawn buggy, they had solid tires, and full-elliptic springs at each corner. Bodywork came in two styles: the Auto-Buggy, which was a surrey with seats for passengers (though the rear ones were removable when loads had to be carried); and the

Auto-Wagon, which was a primitive light truck. Some more conventional touring cars with four-cylinder engines, normal-sized wheels, and pneumatic tires were made in 1910 and 1911, but the high-wheeler was the usually encountered I.H.C. After 1911 and until 1961, I.H.C. went over entirely to commercial vehicles.

23 MAXWELL MODEL HB, 1907, MODEL A, 1909, U.S.A.

When Jonathan Maxwell and Benjamin Briscoe started to make cars in late 1904, they, like so many other American manufacturers, concentrated upon small cars with big, lazy horizontal engines; in this case two twins of 8 h.p. and 15 h.p. They were of modern design, with mechanically-operated inlet valves and shaft drive. Half-elliptic suspension was used. The smaller car had a two-speed epicyclic gear-box, and the larger a three-speed sliding-pinion box. Bore and stroke were 102 × 102 mm. and 127 × 127 mm. respectively, giving 1,668 and 3,219 c.c. They were very popular, particularly after one tied with a Pierce Great Arrow for the Glidden Trophy in their first year of manufacture, and won the Deming Trophy in the same event in 1906. By August 1905, 532 had been built. The 8-h.p. runabout was called the Model L. In 1907 it was renamed the Model LC, with a bore of 114 mm. giving an oversquare engine of 2,060 c.c., and a rating of 12 h.p. The LC could be obtained in RS or RL form, the only difference being a separate or bench seat. The 15 h.p. was continued, as the

four-passenger Model HB (upper illustration). In the same year, the much bigger and more expensive Model D was introduced; but Maxwell made their name with their twins, forming the bulk of the 9,000 cars sold by August 1909. In that year, the LC runabout was enlarged again into the 14-h.p. Model LD; and a new development of the same theme, the Model A, illustrated below, was introduced. Both cars were furnished with a three-speed gear-box, and with full-elliptic springs fore and aft for comfort's sake. Although four-cylinder cars were becoming more and more important in the Maxwell range, the twins were continued until 1912.

24 LAURIN-KLEMENT TYPE B, 1907, 1908, Austria–Hungary (Bohemia)

During the 1890s two Czechs, Vaclav Laurin and Vaclav Klement, started to make the Slavia bicycle; it was a success and paved the way for motor-cycle production, which began in 1899. These, sold under the names of the two partners, were of fine quality and won many racing victories. In 1905, car production began at the Mlada Boleslav works. It was concentrated upon *voiturettes* of the type becoming popular in France: stark and exposed to the elements, but strong, light in weight, cheap to run, low in price, and sporting in behaviour. The Type A was a 6/7 PS water-cooled vee-twin with overhead inlet valves and shaft drive, to which in 1907 was added the bigger 9 PS Type B and 10 PS Type BS.

Types E and F were much bigger bi-bloc fours, the latter being seen often with commercial and taxi bodies, and there was even a straight-eight, but the 6/12 PS Type G of 1908 was another small car, now with a monobloc four-cylinder engine. A derivation, the Type GDV, was much used as a taxi in the capitals of Europe. The type illustrated is the Type B twin, in 1907 and 1908 form. There were twins in the range until 1912. Laurin-Klement cars, like the motor-cycles, became feared in competitions, in the hands of Otto Hieronymus, Count Alexander Kolowrat, and Count Draskovich.

25 ITALA 35/45 h.p., 1907, Italy

Matteo Ceirano's Itala, starting life as a De Dion-engined *voiturette* in 1903, became one of Italy's leading prestige makes in the pre-1914 period. Their heyday was 1904–9, when big, luxurious, fast, expensive machines patterned closely on the fashionable Mercedes design were the rule, starting with an 18 h.p. and a 24 h.p. Their engines had side valves in a T head, pair-cast cylinders, and low-tension magneto ignition, and departed from their German model only in adhering consistently to shaft drive. There were many who said that chain drive was essential for reliability in large, powerful cars; but the Itala proved them decisively wrong when Prince Borghese's 35/45 h.p., shown here, came home first in the transcontinental Peking–Paris Trial of 1907; not to mention wins in the 1905 Coppa Florio, 1906 Targa Florio, and 1907 Coppa della Velocita Races. The Targa Florio was carried off by basically touring 35/45-h.p. cars. The renown won for the make by these successes and others meant fame and patronage extended by the Pope and Queen Margherita of Italy (and therefore, of Italian society). Only F.I.A.T. was a bigger and more famous firm; and it lacked the social *cachet* of the other Turin concern. Not just the transmission but also the engine and chassis were strongly and solidly made, as the Peking–Paris triumph proved. The true power output of the 35/45 h.p. was nearer 60 b.h.p. than 45 from its 7·4 litres, and was developed at the quite high speed of 1,500 r.p.m. (made possible by a short-stroke engine). Maximum speed, even for chassis carrying town car bodies, was around 60 m.p.h. The type was in production from 1907 to 1909, and was the most famous of the Italas.

26 TRIBELHORN PHAETON, 1908, VICTORIA, 1907, Switzerland

The electric car was always a conservative machine, since it was designed primarily for the gentle, silent, smooth progress beloved of the elderly well-to-do when getting about town. Even so, the Tribelhorn, in appearance at least, was more retrograde than most. As can be seen in the illustrations, which are of vehicles dating from 1907 and 1908, this Swiss make catered for a clientèle who still did not accept the motor-car as a new form of transportation in its own right: the bodywork of the two, called a Victoria and a Phaeton respectively, is derived straight from horse-carriage practice, and resembles that worn by cars up to around 1901—not since. The Ateliers Mécaniques A. Tribelhorn started manufacture at Feldbach in 1902, building buses and trucks as well as passenger cars. The 1907 Phaeton had a range of up to 75 miles on one charge, and cruised at 15-20 m.p.h. A single electric motor with a capacity between 40-80 amp/hours was fitted to the passenger cars. After 1919, no more were made, but a small three-wheeler that had just been introduced was very popular with the Swiss Post Office. These were made at a new factory at Altstetten.

27 **PEUGEOT 16 h.p.**
    TYPE 116, 1908,
    7/9 h.p. TYPE 125,
    1911, France

Having achieved the distinction of being the first French manufacturer to put a gasoline-engined car into production (in 1891–2), twenty-nine machines being turned out in that year, Peugeot made no further mark on the motoring scene until Ernest Henry's sensational racing cars arrived in 1912. (This leaves out of consideration the Lion-Peugeots built by Les Fils de Peugeot Frères from 1905 to 1910.) In between, the firm became known for well-built, unadventurous touring cars based carefully on other people's known and tried lines: indeed, the very first Peugeot was mostly Panhard et Levassor. Still following fashion, it began to make Mercedes-pattern vehicles late in 1901, with the 15 h.p. of late 1901 and the 12 h.p. of 1902; the latter car had

mechanically-operated valves, honeycomb radiator, and channel-steel frame. By 1908 (upper illustration), there was a fully representative and normal range of middle-class machinery with one, two, four, or six cylinders, and chain or shaft drive according to size, which extended from an 8-h.p. twin to a 50-h.p. monster. The car shown is the 16-h.p. Type 116, with 2·2-litre, four-cylinder side-valve engine, high-tension magneto ignition, a four-speed gearbox and shaft drive: a totally conventional recipe that worked very well. The lower illustration shows the Type 125 7/9-h.p. twin of similar general specification, and 1·1 litres; but by this time monobloc engines of L-head configuration had arrived; the 1908 car still used a T head and pair-cast cylinders.

28 **BRASIER TYPE VL,**
    1908, France

By 1908, when the car shown was built, the Société des Automobiles Brasier of Ivry-Port, whose name had become world-famous through their racing successes, had shot their bolt. That year saw their last participation in any *grande épreuve*—the French Grand Prix. From now on, they lived on the reputation gained in two wins in the 1904 and 1905 Gordon Bennett Races (under their former name of Richard-Brasier), and on that of their solid, well made, conventional touring machines such as the Type VL of 10/12 CV illustrated. This car was the last of the two-cylinder Brasiers, and was current until 1911 alongside heavier metal. In time, their layout became conservative—in 1912, some models still had exposed valve gear and pair-cast cylinders. Their name was that of Henri Brasier, their designer from 1902, formerly of Mors. The 'Richard' half of the earlier name was gradually dropped after 1905, when Georges Richard, founder of the company, left to make the Unic car (although the vehicle shown still bears it).

29 ADAMS 10 h.p., 1908, Great Britain

The Adams Manufacturing Company of Bedford was probably the first British concern to impart the American concept of simple, foolproof motoring into a home-produced (if not home-designed) car. Edward Hewitt, who made cars under his own name in the United States, designed the Adams as well, and in recognition of this, the first few were called Adams-Hewitts. The massive, slow-running, centrally mounted, horizontal single-cylinder engine of the original Adams-Hewitt of 1906, its three-speed epicyclic gearing, its single-chain drive and its suspension by one long spring on each side joining front and rear axles, were all typically American. The 'Adams Improved Planetary Gear' was actuated by pedals alone, giving rise to the slogan 'Pedals to Push, That's All'. The 10-h.p. engine had cylinder dimensions of 121 × 152 mm., providing 1,750 c.c. A variation on the original 10 h.p. was offered from 1908, when a long-wheelbase car with three-quarter elliptic front springs and full-elliptics at the rear was introduced. One of each type is illustrated. There was a twin by that time, and

fours followed until production ceased in 1914. The singles had gone out of production four years earlier. The most exciting Adams was undoubtedly the vee-eight of 1906–9, of which the power unit was based on the Antoinette aero engine. Front-wheel brakes were optional, and a compressed-air self-starter was available. Eleven of these remarkable cars were said to have been sold. The last two features were advertised on the normal four-cylinder Adams of 1910 as well. All models except the single had vertical engines and shaft drive. About 3,000 Adamses were made in all.

30 LANCHESTER 20 h.p., 1908, Great Britain

The Lanchester Engine Company made its name with its 10-h.p. and 12-h.p. horizontally-opposed twins, which could be bought from 1900 until as late as 1908. The air-cooled 10 h.p. two-cylinder was notably quiet and smooth for its type, the car's handling was extremely good, thanks to very accurate steering and its rigid body-cum-chassis, its performance was excellent, and the cantilever springing front and rear was very comfortable. Its fame was due not only to the way in which it motored, but also to its extreme unconventionality of design, which inhibited its popularity. The first steps away from the earliest production design were taken in 1904, when an over-square four with vertical cylinders in line was introduced. This 20 h.p. (illustrated here in 1908 form) was supplemented by a 28-h.p. six in 1906, and the two cars were current until 1910 and 1911 respectively. Maximum speed was 50 m.p.h. in open form, which was good for a tourer of only 2½ litres. Power output was 28 b.h.p. at 2,200 r.p.m. (a high engine speed for 1904). Although the engine of the Lanchester (by now with horizontal overhead valves) had moved forward from its original central situation to a position between the front-seat passengers, it still had a wick carburettor, and the car was still almost without a hood. However, the controls began to be modified for wider acceptance. The epicyclic gear-box was retained, but while the 20 h.p. had the classic Lanchester side-lever steering, in 1911 this was to be replaced by a steering wheel (which had been optional since 1907). The Lanchester remained an expensive and sophisticated machine for the luxury market, its simplification being aimed at widening its acceptance mainly among chauffeurs (who so often influenced their employers' choice of car); but its renown spread, thanks to a very distinguished roll of customers, including British and Indian nobility.

31 BENTALL 16/20 h.p., 1908, Great Britain

East Anglia, then as now a predominantly agricultural part of England, nevertheless spawned a local motor industry of quite considerable proportions, most of it supported regionally, in the first decades of the century. Commonly, as in the case of E. H. Bentall & Company of Maldon in Essex, an engineering firm already established in some other field, in this case agricultural machinery and most recently stationary engines, would make cars as a sideline. Bentall did so from 1906 to 1913. Their designer, Edmund Ernest Bentall, planned four models, two being twins of 8 h.p. and 11 h.p., and two fours of 16 h.p. and 16/20 h.p. The cars illustrated are of the last-named type. It (and the 11 h.p.) were unusual in one major respect: the engine, with a bore and stroke of 100 × 95 mm., was over-square. Apart from this and an exceptionally easy gear-change, the Bentall was a solid, reliable, unspectacular machine of the kind one might expect from its antecedents. The engine had a T-head layout, with separately-cast cylinders and high-tension magneto ignition, driving through a three-speed gear-box and cardan shaft to a live axle. The engine's odd dimensions and separate cylinders caused the car's demise, for it suffered under a horsepower tax based on bore size, and was old-fashioned at a time when pair-cast cylinders were normal and monobloc castings on their way in. Retooling was not practical for such a small output, so car production ceased. Most of the car was made by Bentall, and most of the bodies were from local coachbuilders in Chelmsford and Colchester. Around 100 Bentalls were made, the 16/20 h.p. being the most popular model.

32 SCHACHT, 1908, U.S.A.

Like the I.H.C. (22), the Schacht from Cincinnati was one of the breed of 'high-wheelers' which proliferated briefly in the Middle West before the farmer who wanted something more civilized and orthodox for expeditions to town and for 'visiting' could buy a

Model T Ford (47), which would do the same hard work. The Schacht, though fundamentally similar to the I.H.C., differed in certain technical respects. The 10/12-h.p. engine, which was smaller (1·6 litres), rear-mounted, and had side valves, was water-cooled always, with a front-mounted radiator. There was friction-disc primary drive, and the suspension was on 'gas-buggy' lines, with a single very long cantilever spring each side. Steering was always by wheel. As with the I.H.C., the engine used a horizontally-opposed layout, with coil ignition, and final drive was by side-chains. The Schacht was made from 1905 to 1908 in this form; thereafter, like I.H.C., they tried to recapture their disappearing market by offering more normal, four-cylinder cars, but were unable to do so. From 1914 they turned to trucks alone, after the manner of the Akron firm, surviving until 1938.

33 WHITE 30 h.p., 1908, U.S.A.

After the Stanley brothers (76), Rollin H. White was the most successful maker of steam cars in the world. White was a sewing-machine manufacturer, like a number of others who were turning to cars at around the same time (1901): the second biggest in the world. From the start, the automotive product of the White Sewing Machine Company was a more sophisticated machine than the Stanley. It followed French Serpollet principles with its efficient flash generator which produced instantaneous superheated steam. The system was quick and safe, and the

steam was easily controlled. A condenser was fitted from the beginning. The first little buggy-like Stanhope model of 1901-2 had a twin-cylinder 6-h.p. double-acting simple engine, replaced by a compound engine in 1903. This now lived in front, under a hood, in order that the White should resemble gasoline cars, and there was shaft drive to a live axle. The 'radiator' was in fact the condenser. By 1905 the firm's name had been changed to White & Company, and a two-speed gear provided. The 15 h.p. was boosted to 18 h.p. in 1906 and to 20 h.p. the following year, when a second type was introduced for the first time: this was the 30 h.p. illustrated in 1908 form. The 30 h.p. lasted only until 1909, being superseded by a 40 h.p., but this in turn, and the 20 h.p., was dead after 1911, for in the previous year the White Company decided to go over to gasoline-engined cars completely. (The writing had been on the wall two years before, when a gasoline car based on the French Delahaye was shown to the public.) From 1901 White boosted sales of their touring cars with a string of convincing victories in competitions not only in the United States (mainly in the hands of Webb Jay), but also in Britain, where an 18 h.p. made fastest time of the day at the Shelsley Walsh hillclimb in 1906.

34 STEARNS 45/90 h.p., 1908, U.S.A.

The F. B. Stearns Company made cars from 1899, the first being typical American runabouts with large, slow-turning single (later two-) cylinder engines. However, in the period under consideration in this book the firm was known for fast, well-made and expensive machines. The earliest of these came in 1905, when in company with so many other manufacturers the world over, the company went over to the Mercedes pattern, which led in the luxury class. The basic machine was a four-cylinder car with mechanically-operated inlet valves, pair-cast cylinders, and double side-chain drive. The colossal 13-litre car shown, the six-cylinder 45/90 h.p. of 1908, was capable of between 80 and 90 m.p.h. and was regarded as the fastest American production car of its day. Ball-bearings were used throughout. It was built to special order, costing $6,250 (£1,250) in 1908. Few were made, since this was extremely expensive even by European standards. Smaller models had the option of chain or shaft drive. Later, after Frank B. Stearns left, the Stearns became more sedate, adopting the Knight sleeve-valve engine, in which form it was known as the Stearns-Knight and was built until 1930.

35   GAGGENAU TYP 60, 1907, TYP D 10-18, 1908, Germany

The Suddeutsche Automobil Fabrik of Gaggenau came into existence in 1904, when the car-building activities of the Bergmann's Industriewerke (founded in 1889) were separated from the parent firm. These had begun in 1895, when Theodor Bergmann's engineer, Josef Vollmer, had designed the Orient Express car for him. This was a belt-driven machine of Benz type, notable

only for its very early use of low-tension magneto ignition. From 1902 to 1904 Bergmann progressed to better things; *voiturettes* with one cylinder and 5 to 7 PS, twins of 10 and 12 PS, and a 16 PS four, all called Bergmanns. The first cars of the independent concern were the single-cylinder friction-drive Liliput *voiturettes* designed by Willi Seck. They were current until 1907, but before then, some much heavier metal had appeared. Two big, conventional, bi-bloc fours were introduced in 1905; the 18/22 PS of four litres with a T head, and the six-litre L-head 24/36 PS. They had magneto ignition, three forward speeds, and shaft drive. From 1908, smaller L-head monobloc fours joined the catalogued range. The machine illustrated at the bottom is a 1908 Typ D 10-18, current until 1910, developing 20 b.h.p. at 1,600 r.p.m. and capable of rather over 40 m.p.h. with 2·6 litres. There was dual ignition. Very different were the Typ 35 and Typ 60, big machines of advanced specification, with their single overhead-camshaft engines that developed (respectively) 55 b.h.p. from 4·7 litres and 75 b.h.p. from 8·8 litres. The Typ 35 used shaft drive, and the Typ 60 chains (the only Gaggenau to do so). Some were fitted with sports bodies, but others were roomier styles such as that shown at top. A 1907 Typ 60 is illustrated. The model was listed from 1906 to 1910. Even fiercer were the special cars designed for competitions. Gaggenaus were seen in all the most important events of 1906–10, from the Kaiserpreis race of 1907 and the Herkomer and Prince Henry trials, to the Czar's Cup. They were achieving successes as late as the post-war years, even though production had ended with the turning over of the factory to commercial vehicle production by Benz at the end of 1910. That company had acquired a controlling interest three years earlier.

36 LANCIA TIPO 51 ALFA, 1908, Italy

Vincenzo Lancia, the celebrated FIAT racing driver, turned to motor manufacture in 1907. His first works was damaged by fire, so the earliest car to bear his name emerged from an Itala factory (25). It was a completely orthodox machine with four pair-cast cylinders and side valves in a T head. Like the Itala, the Lancia used shaft drive, never chains. It was of excellent quality, and gained a reputation for smoothness and reliability. The cubic capacity of $2\frac{1}{2}$ litres was said to produce 53 b.h.p. The short stroke helped the attainment of a high engine speed (1,800 r.p.m.) and hence of an exceptional power output for the size of engine, but this figure is excessive. The Fabbrica Automobili Lancia claimed only 25–28 b.h.p., which is more likely, and creditable for 1908. The higher output may have been that of the Alfas specially prepared for racing, one of which won the light car race at Savannah, Georgia, in the same year. Larger, monobloc engines followed in succeeding years. The original car was the Tipo 51 or Alfa, and those that came after it, until the Lambda of 1922, were also called after Greek letters of the alphabet. The Alfa's companion six, an obscure machine, was called the Dialfa: until the end of the 1920s the firm was best known for its fours.

37 FIAT 18/24 h.p., 1908, Italy

The first Fiat car was put into production in 1899, and was a modern *voiturette* of conventional type, with a rear-mounted horizontal twin-cylinder engine of $3\frac{1}{2}$ h.p. Twins were made until 1902, but a four-cylinder chain-driven car based on the German Mercedes had appeared in the previous year. The engine was at the front, and had a honeycomb radiator; but until the end of 1902 the inlet valves were automatic. This 12 h.p. was soon supplemented by bigger 16-h.p. and 24-h.p. models. These three cars of 1902 set the Fiat trend for the next six years: big, fast, expensive cars of fine quality, all made on the same orthodox lines— four cylinders cast in pairs; side valves in a T head; four forward speeds; and chain drive (which was the rule for all models until 1906). The 18/24 h.p. shown, introduced in 1907, was in fact the last Fiat to have a bi-bloc engine; its successors were all cast monobloc. It was also the first to use high-tension instead of low-tension magneto ignition. The cubic capacity was $4\frac{1}{2}$ litres, producing a conservative 24 b.h.p. at 1,200 r.p.m. This sufficed to give a maximum speed of 45 m.p.h. with formal bodywork.

38 GERMAIN 18/22 h.p., 1908, Belgium

The Ateliers Germain of Monceau-sur-Sambre, founded in 1897, produced their first car in the following year. It was the Daimler from Germany made under licence; the two-cylinder

6-h.p. Phönix type of 1896, which Germain supplemented by a 12-h.p. four. A few years later, in 1901, the 'Daimler Belge' was a car on French Panhard et Levassor lines. This was not much of a departure, since the Panhard, of Daimler origin and in turn providing the basis of the improved Daimlers of 1896, was not to diverge greatly from them until late in the same year of 1901. In 1903 Germain built their first original design, the 15/18 h.p. Its L-head engine was very modern for the time, and had dual ignition. Otherwise, the car was similar to the Panhard. However, 1904 saw the adoption of Mercedes-type pressed-steel frames and honeycomb radiators, and the largest of the range, the 35 h.p., wore the handsome oval radiator that was to become Germain's trademark. These cars, still chain-driven, had four forward speeds and made the firm's reputation for fine engineering. With 1905 came shaft drive and a live axle in the most famous Germain type, the 14/22-h.p. 'Chainless'. It reverted to a T-head engine and had three forward speeds, but was very fast for its size (three litres), and gained a name in competitions. The cylinders were separately cast. In 1907 there followed a larger version of the same car, the 18/22 h.p., with a bigger bore (102 mm. instead of 92 mm.) giving 3·6 litres. This is the machine illustrated; it was made until 1914 with few changes, so good was the basic 1905 design.

39 AJAX 8/16 CV, 1908, Switzerland

From 1906 to 1910, Gottfried Aigner of Zurich made his Ajax, which was always a four-cylinder machine, and generally, though not exclusively, seen as a taxicab. Being extraordinarily strong as well as refined in the manner of their going, they were suited to such use: but they were also seen in racing: the Targa Florio of 1907, and Swiss events. The chain drive of the first chassis gave way to shaft drive on the smallest model of the three made from 1907, the four-cylinder, 2·3-litre Type A 8/16 CV shown, or to an option of chains or shaft on the larger, the four- and six-cylinder 24 CV. The cylinders were cast monobloc, except on the six, where they were in threes, and there were four forward speeds. Later, a 50 CV six was also offered. All Ajaxes had side valves. For 1910, the 8/16 CV and its companions were to be dropped in favour of two new models, but the company died before they could appear. With the landaulet body illustrated, the 8/16 CV was capable of between 35 and 40 m.p.h.

40 RENAULT MODEL AX, 1909, France

The name of Renault was made by their *voiturette* of 1899, which was the first car to combine shaft drive with a sprung live axle. These features, and its front engine, friction clutch and gear-box with direct drive on top, became the model for all modern small cars in the early 1900s. Renault themselves dropped the *voiturette* in 1902, having progressed to bigger cars (12); but in 1906 they reintroduced a small car into the range that was to bring them almost as much fame. This differed in being completely conventional in its time, if thoroughly up to date, with two monobloc cylinders, side valves in an L head, three speeds, shaft drive (of course), and the robustness, longevity, and refinement that were now trade-marks of the make, and shared with the other, larger models. The little car was made in 8 CV (75 × 120 mm., 1,060 c.c.) and 9 CV (80 × 120 mm., 1,204 c.c.) form until 1914, and because of its low running costs and reliability, was seen in its thousands not only in passenger-car use, but also pulling commercial and taxi bodies. The idio-syncratic tumbler-action gear-box did not affect its popularity; this was guaranteed mainly by the car's com-parative smoothness and quietness com-pared with most other small cars of the time. The type shown, the first Model AX, was made from 1908 to 1912; it used the 8 CV engine. The indicated power was developed at 1,200 r.p.m. The terminology of these twins is very complex. Briefly and simply, apart from the AX there were (among the 8 CV types) the BQ of 1912 (also made in 9 CV form), and the 1912 CX. The 9 CVs were the 1913 type AX, the EK of 1913–14, and the DL of 1914 only. Yet other designations were applied to taxicabs.

41 **HUMBER 8 h.p.**, 1909, Great Britain

The early history of Humber of Coventry is a chequered one. It began with Thomas Humber's fine bicycles, which he started to make in 1868, but the name suffered during a spell of four years, 1896–1900, when it formed part

of the shaky empire of the company promoter H. J. Lawson, wherein it made only a handful of vehicles, and those of low quality. The Breton Louis Coatalen, later to make his name with Sunbeam (88), became designer in 1901, and Humber Ltd. rose from the wreck of Lawson's dreams to make a new reputation for excellent, low-priced, small to medium-sized vehicles of modern, if conventional design. The first to be truly popular was the single-cylinder shaft-driven Humberette of 1903–5, and until the latter year there was also the Humber Olympia Tandem, a motor tricycle that was also a success. The Humberette, like many of the make from 1903 to 1908, was made in two versions in two factories—the de luxe Beeston Humbers at a works in the Nottinghamshire town of that name, and the cheaper Coventry Humbers in Warwickshire. Coatalen's 12 h.p. small four of 1902 was another cheap but good car that had the refinement of a four-speed gear-box, although retaining the tubular frame of the Humberette. From 1905 to 1908 almost nothing but fours was made, these including the well-liked 16/20-h.p. Beeston Humber and 15-h.p. Coventry Humber, both with steel frames; but in 1908 the company bid again for the voiturette market with the 8 h.p. illus-trated, which was current until 1910. This had a $1\frac{1}{2}$-litre, two-cylinder engine of unusual smoothness for its type, with full-pressure lubrication, and the added luxuries of dual ignition and Humber's own detachable wheels. There was a three-speed sliding-pinion gear-box, and shaft drive to a live axle. Weight was a modest 14 cwt., and top speed 40 m.p.h., which was very creditable.

42 ALLDAYS & ONIONS
10/12 h.p., 1909,
Great Britain

By the early years of the twentieth century, the products of the very old-established engineering firm of Allday & Onions, founded in 1650, were varied and ubiquitous: about the time when the car shown was motoring about Britain's roads, an Alldays & Onions anvil was giving good service to other, broken-down motorists in a remote village forge in distant Ethiopia. They were making principally pneumatic equipment at the time when they diversified further into motor vehicles, in 1898. They became known for massive commercial and public service chassis, but their best-known passenger cars were small, economical, and low-priced—and also good, soundly-made and reliable, if not very refined in their manner of going (though this was not expected of cars of the type in the first decade of the century). After building their primitive but effective Traveller, which could be had either as a tandem two-seater or as a salesman's box-van (and lacked reverse gear, differential, and rear springs), the company offered a 'proper car', still with single-cylinder engine. It was followed in 1905 by the twin-cylinder car shown (in 1909 form), which was quieter and smoother. This 10/12 h.p. followed the Alldays tradition in being popular with commercial travellers, and was also frequently seen as a light van. It was made until 1912.

43 COOPER, 1909,
Great Britain

The Cooper, like the Bentall (31), was a product of East Anglia's once-thriving automobile industry; in this case made by the Cooper Steam Digger Company Ltd. of King's Lynn, Norfolk. They made, hired out, and undertook contract work with agricultural machinery, including engines. In 1908 Ralph Lucas asked them to make a batch of fifty Valveless cars, which had two-stroke engines (56). He ultimately took this business elsewhere, but Thomas Cooper then turned to cars himself. The first had two-cylinder two-stroke engines, transversely mounted and inclined, with chain primary and final drive. A shaft-driven four-cylinder piston-valve two-stroke car followed, its engine conventionally mounted. Other peculiarities were the two-speed axle and the rear suspension, which was far ahead of its time in that it was adjustable according to load. Unequal cantilever springs (which looked like long quarter-elliptics) were linked by a transverse cantilever spring which could be brought into play by a finger adjustment. The odd engine worked very well, the six cars built being capable of upwards of 50 m.p.h., which was creditable for 1909–10.

44 RILEY 10 h.p., 1909,
Great Britain

William Riley's Riley Cycle Company, formed in 1896, progressed three years later to motor tricars and quadricycles, followed by motor bicycles. They used proprietary engines, mostly by De Dion. Then the Riley Engine Company, a separate concern founded by Percy Riley in 1903, began to make engines for Riley vehicles, and also for other manufacterers. The tricar of 1904 was more sophisticated than most of its spidery breed, with its two-speed sliding-pinion gear-box and friction clutch, $4\frac{1}{2}$-h.p. water-cooled single-cylinder engine with mechanically-operated inlet valve, and bucket seat instead of the more usual saddle. This tricar was further refined into an extremely popular 6 h.p. or 9 h.p. model with vee-twin engine, three-speed gear-box, wheel steering, car-type horizontal chassis frame, and leaf spring front and coil spring rear suspension. These machines were fast, comfortable, and easy to handle. 1906 saw the first Riley four-wheeler car, powered by one of Percy's 9-h.p. 90-degree vee-twin units, transversely mounted, mated to the same three-speed transmission found on the tricar. Indeed, but for the fact that the extra wheel allowed side-by-side seating, and a front radiator was fitted, these things giving a more car-like appearance, the little machine was the same as the tricar. In 1908 the car grew up a little more. The vee-twin engine, now larger (10 h.p.) was brought forward from the centre to the front, under a hood with an elegant oval radiator, and there was shaft drive. This is the type illustrated. There was also a still bigger 12/18-h.p. vee-twin of nearly two litres capacity, current since 1907. The Riley Cycle Company was also responsible, in 1907, for a pattern of detachable wire wheel that had been adopted as an optional extra by as many as 183 car makers by 1912.

45 AUSTIN 7 h.p., 1909, Great Britain

In 1905, Herbert Austin left Wolseley after that company abandoned the horizontal-engined cars for which he had made them famous; though when he set up on his own, in the following year, he went as conventional as anyone, with vertical four- and six-cylinder units. History becomes complicated after 1908, for the English-built version of the French Gladiator also came to be made in the Austin works, while (in the 1909–11 period) the 7 h.p. model in the range of Swift of Coventry was also built as an Austin in the Swift factory. The Gladiator looked very much an Austin, and the Swift was called an Austin and given an Austin radiator. This is the car illustrated; a single-cylinder *voiturette* of the type common at the time. It weighed under half a ton and cost only £150 (then $750), but until the coming of the 'proper' Seven, Herbert Austin made his money with solid, medium- to large-sized family tourers (69). It is doubly misleading to call it the 'first Austin Seven': it was not only no relation to the advanced little four-cylinder light car of 1922 in the technical sense—it was no relation by blood, either, for it was made by Swift only, and also appeared as a Swift, with a Swift radiator.

46 VAUXHALL 12/16 h.p., 1909, Great Britain

The first four-cylinder car to be made by the Vauxhall Ironworks followed closely on the heels of the 1905–6 three-cylinder machine (4), the first being the 3·3-litre 18/20 h.p. of late 1905. It had been introduced while the three-cylinder was current, but it was so much better liked that the former was withdrawn. After the firm's move to Luton (where it is today) in 1905, the next major event was the formation of Vauxhall Motors Ltd. two years later, to handle car manufacture only: the former company had been responsible for the marine engines as well, but the expansion of the car side of the business dictated the split. The 18/20 h.p. was a popular model; but the smaller, less well-known 12/16 h.p. illustrated followed in 1906. Its 80 × 110 mm. engine (the same dimensions as the three-cylinder) provided 2,212 c.c., and there were three forward speeds. As with the 18/20 h.p., there were side valves in a T head and pair-cast cylinders. The later 18/20s abandoned chain drive, the remaining vestige of the first Vauxhall design, and the 12/16 h.p. had shaft drive from the beginning. Laurence Pomeroy's first design for Vauxhall, the famous and highly-efficient L-head 16/20 h.p. of 1908 that won the Two Thousand Miles Trial and was developed into the Prince Henry series, overshadowed the two T-head fours from the start, good cars though they were.

47 FORD MODEL T, 1909, U.S.A.

By 1908 Henry Ford was already established as a large motor manufacturer by the standards of the time, thanks largely to his successful Model N. However, his aim was to produce an automobile sufficiently low-priced to sell to the mass market, and attractive in other ways too: simple and of good quality, for reliability; and easy to drive. Others,

notably Oldsmobile and Rambler in the United States and Darracq in France, had tried to break through to the masses as early as 1901–2, and had achieved exceptional sales for their time, but now, when Ford and his backers took the plunge, the circumstances were more promising—usable roads were less rare, motor-cars had lost much of their reputation as eccentric and temperamental toys for the wealthy (thanks to their increased numbers and reliability), and design had stabilized: an exceedingly important consideration, since to be made in mass quantities at a low price, any product had to remain in production for a substantial period. The man and the circumstances together produced the world's first mass-appeal, mass-selling car: the Model T Ford. For the sake of economy, all other models were dropped. Gradually, as the gamble paid off and the demand grew, the methods necessary to mass-production were applied to the new car. They were not all new, having been applied in America to guns, watches, and, to an extent, to motor-cars. As Henry M. Leland of Cadillac had already preached and practised, parts were standardized and interchangeable, thanks to precision in manufacture. This precision was attained not by the inefficient handwork, but by machine work, which in turn called for the development of specialized machine tools.

Mechanically, the Model T achieved its objectives without departing very much from standard American practice. It was powered by a four-cylinder, L-head engine of 2·9 litres. Power output was about 20 b.h.p., which was more or less in line with contemporary practice in 1908 (*see* Introduction). Yet, since the car was so light, and a high final-drive ratio thereby made possible, it was both economical on fuel and had a good turn of speed: 40 m.p.h. or a little more. Low weight and good low-speed torque made for exceptionally good acceleration, too. A four-cylinder engine, with its comparative smoothness and power, was a luxury in the Model T's price range. Until now, buyers had had to put up with the roughness and inflexibility inherent in most two-cylinder runabouts. As in the Model N, there were only two forward speeds and reverse, obtained through an epicyclic gear-box. Thereby, costs were cut, and the gear-shifting bogy, the most alarming confronting the new motorist, had most of its teeth drawn. The excellent low-speed pulling power of the engine helped. Lightness, high ground clearance, and a good steering lock helped to make sure of the car's popularity in rural areas where roads were bad or non-existent. The Model T's price at the beginning of its first model year, 1909, was $825 (£165); less than any other four-cylinder car on the market, and less, even, than most of the inferior two-cylinder cars. At the outset of its career, the Ford's disadvantages were few. Its equipment was exceptionally scanty, and its clever fly-wheel generator, which provided current for the trembler coils, was sometimes reluctant to start the car before the cranker exhausted himself. But the criterion was surely sales. 11,000 units were sold in the first model year; a tenth of the whole American industry's output. Ten years later Ford was building 3,000 Model T's a day, and the car remained in production in modified form until 1927.

48 CHALMERS-DETROIT MODEL F, 1909, U.S.A.

The name of Chalmers dates from 1907, when Hugh Chalmers acquired an interest in, and became head of, the E. R. Thomas-Detroit Company, which had made cars under the name of Thomas-Detroit. (E. R. Thomas was also responsible for the Thomas car (21) of Buffalo.) The car was renamed Chalmers-Detroit, and in 1911 became the Chalmers. From the beginning, it was entered in competitions with a remarkable degree of success, and although the engines used were not particularly big, they produced notably more power for their size than most in the United States at the time, which relied on sheer size for their punch. Until 1913, all were fours. The secret lay in their high-revving capabilities, attained partly by the use of overhead valves and a short-stroke engine. Indeed, the 40-h.p. model was 'over-square', with cylinder dimensions of 127 × 121 mm. The Chalmers was very early in the field in the United States in using a monobloc engine, which permitted a shorter, stiffer crankshaft, which in turn helped to allow high revolutions. The engine was made in unit with the gear-box; another very modern feature. Maximum speed of the 30 h.p. in normal touring form was 50 m.p.h., a high figure for a car of the period with a medium-sized engine. The 30-h.p. Model F Chalmers-Detroit of 1909 that is illustrated had a cubic capacity of

3·7 litres, high-tension magneto ignition, and shaft drive, like its bigger stablemate. 1,200 of the 30 h.p. were in use by 1909, and the model was still current in 1911.

49 PREMIER 40 h.p., 1909, 1910, U.S.A.

The Premier from Indianapolis, made from 1903 to 1925 in passenger-car form and as a taxicab for another two years, started life as a very modern machine with four pair-cast cylinders in a T head, steel frame, mechanically-operated inlet valves, sliding-pinion gear-box and shaft drive, rather like the Itala from Italy (25). There was a brief flirtation in 1905 with an air-cooled four designed by G. A. Weidely of proprietary engine fame (who also designed the more conventional models), but water-cooling was the rule. The cars shown, of 1909 and 1910, are both of 40-h.p. type, with a bore and stroke of 114 × 133 mm., and a capacity of 5·4 litres. Ignition was by coil and high-tension magneto. In the latter year, there was also a 60-h.p. six, identical except for the number of cylinders. Bore and stroke were the same. It was the biggest car in that year's Glidden Tour, and won it outright. A 40-h.p. Premier was fourth. The car was notable for its full-elliptic suspension fore and aft.

50 OPEL 4/8 PS, 1909, Germany

The Adam Opel Motorwagenfabrik had its origins in sewing-machine manufacture, which started in 1862. Bicycles followed, and in 1898, the first Opel-built car, which was a simple belt-driven machine on Benz lines that had been sold as the Lutzmann by an independent concern from 1894 until taken over by Opel four years later. By 1901 this type was obsolete, and Opel turned to the Darracq from France for their next inspiration, importing Darracq chassis and fitting German bodies. This proved a great success, for Darracq were pioneering quantity production of the first really practical small car that was also cheap. These single-cylinder Opels had front-mounted vertical engines with variable-lift inlet valves, driving through a cone clutch, three-speed sliding-pinion gear-box and cardan shaft to a live rear axle. Opel-Darracqs were sold until 1906, but a native product was developed from them. In fact, the first 'independent' Opels dated from 1902; a twin and a four, with mechanically-operated inlet valves. The latter also had an L-head layout and magneto ignition; a modern specification which was common to all the German-designed cars by 1905. Darracq types were made alongside them. By 1905, there were four Opel-Darracqs and three true Opels in the range, but in 1906 the connection with the Suresnes firm was severed. The smallest of the 'German' cars, the 8/14 PS (later 12/14 PS) twin, was a robust and reliable little car that became known as the Doktorwagen. This name was also given to the smaller 6/12 PS twin that replaced it in 1908, and to the machine shown, the 4/8 PS of 1909, which had a four-cylinder engine of 1,128 c.c., and developed its 8 b.h.p. at 1,600 r.p.m. Like all Opels, it was a modern design, now with monobloc engine.

51 **MARTINI 12/16 CV,**
1909, 1911, Switzerland

Friedrich von Martini was best known to the world at large for his rifles, but he also made machinery for the textile industry, and from 1880 built stationary engines intended for the same use. The first gasoline engine came in 1889. When in 1897 the rifle patent became void, Adolf von Martini, Friedrich's son, turned to motor vehicle manufacture to replace it. In this he succeeded: thirty cars were built in 1902, 100 in 1903, and 130 in 1904. This growth necessitated a new factory, which was built at St. Blaise and devoted to cars. The company was British-controlled from 1906 to 1908. 1909, the year of the car shown in the upper illustration, saw 260 chassis turned out by the company. Two years later, however, it was in financial difficulties. The Martini was always a beautifully made machine on the most modern lines: even the 1897 car had magneto ignition, and the firm's first four, of 1902, had cylinders in vee formation. Even when it went conventional, building cars to the French Rochet-Schneider pattern (67) in 1903, a thoroughly up-to-date type was chosen. It was based on the German Mercedes, with mechanically-operated inlet valves and honeycomb radiator (though retaining an armoured-wood frame). The model shown is the 12/16 CV, of 1909 (top) and 1911 (bottom). This was an almost entirely orthodox 2·2-litre machine

with four cylinders cast monobloc, overhead inlet valves, four forward speeds and shaft drive.

52 **DELAUNAY-BELLEVILLE TYPE HB,**
1911, **TYPE H,** 1910,
France

The Delaunay-Belleville not only had the most distinguished-sounding name of any French car, it lived up to it in the metal, for it was the finest luxury car produced in France before 1914. Like most machines in that class in that age, the first of the breed, that appeared at the Paris Salon of 1904, was completely orthodox in specification. The designer was Marius Barbarou. Quietness, flexibility, refinements of design such as an all-enveloping undertray and full-pressure lubrication, and the peerless quality of its engineering singled the car out. It had four cylinders cast separately, and there were side valves in a T head. The smallest of the first range could be had with shaft drive; the rest were only available chain-driven. The smooth running of both fours and sixes owed itself in part to the very short, rigid crankshafts used. For the 1908 season, the first six-cylinder cars arrived. The most popular of the sixes started life as the Type H of 15 CV introduced that year. It is shown in 1910 Type H and 1911 Type HB form. Its cylinders, at first cast in threes, were pair-cast by 1911. The valves were in an L-head layout, and cubic capacity was 4·1 and 4·4 litres. There was shaft drive, as on all catalogued models from 1911.

53 HOTCHKISS TYPE T, 1910, France

The name of Hotchkiss does not sound French, and is not: it was the name of an American weapons manufacturer who came to France and helped to arm the Emperor Napoleon III's forces during the Franco-Prussian War. The S.A. des Anciens Etablissements Hotchkiss became known for their light quick-firing guns, including machine-guns; by 1903 they were in low water, and turned to motor manufacture to save themselves. Their first models were two fours, of 18 h.p. and 35 h.p. Their engines were T-head side valves, with pair-cast cylinders and low-tension magneto ignition. Hotchkiss cars were beautifully made, refined and expensive machines at the same time solid, reliable, and long-lived. They also introduced Hotchkiss drive to the motoring world; the system by which the torque of the exposed propeller-shaft was taken by the rear springs. Hotchkiss never offered a chain-driven car. From 1908 the design was both simplified and modernized, and smaller cars made their appearance. The ball-bearing crank of the first cars gave way to a plain-bearing component, and most engines were henceforth of mono-bloc construction, with forced lubrication. The model illustrated, the Type T of 16/20 CV, was one of the new type with a side-valve L-head four-cylinder engine of 3·1 litres (95 × 110 mm.).

54 DEASY 12 h.p., 1910, Great Britain

The Deasy Motor Car Manufacturing Company was founded in 1906, and remained distinct until 1912, when following a takeover by the Siddeley Autocar company three years before, it was renamed the Siddeley-Deasy Motor Car Company. Captain H. H. P. Deasy is probably better known to the historian for his success in promoting other makes that he sold but did not make, such as the Martini from Switzerland, but in 1906 he turned to manufacture with the first car bearing his name. Called the 24 h.p., it was unusual for its day in several ways. The armoured-wood frame was old-fashioned by then, but the L-head monobloc engine (four cylinders, $4\frac{1}{2}$ litres) was very modern in concept, while the front suspension by a single transverse spring was rare in so large a car.

The engine developed 24 b.h.p. at 1,000 r.p.m. dual ignition was provided, and there were four forward speeds and shaft drive to a live axle. The design was by E. W. Lewis, formerly of Daimler and Rover. This type was made until 1910. By that year, however, when the car shown was built, Deasy had gone over to a dashboard radiator with some models, as was fashionable. This reflected the influence of J. D. Siddeley, who had taken over in 1909. The new types were conventional cars, with steel frames, made in two sizes: the 14/20 h.p. and the bigger 18/28 h.p. In late 1910, they were joined by the 12 h.p. illustrated. This was a pleasant small tourer of 2 litres, with the option of three or four forward speeds, and a worm-drive rear axle. A change of name took place, and from late 1912 the cars were known as Siddeley-Deasys.

55 AC SOCIABLE, 1910, Great Britain

John Weller of Weller Brothers Ltd., financed by John Portwine, a butcher, had already made a full-sized car under his own name when, in 1904, he began to build a powered delivery tricycle for tradesmen, with a box for goods between the front wheels, called the Autocarrier. Three years later a seat for a second passenger could be had instead of the box, bringing the little vehicle into line with the tricar type that was popular at the time as the next best thing to a motor-cycle. Like Riley (44), Autocarriers Ltd. improved the recipe by providing two side-by-side seats in their AC Sociable introduced in 1909, shown here, but unlike the Coventry firm, they retained a three-wheeler configuration for longer. The engine was a centrally-mounted, transverse, air-cooled single-cylinder unit of 649 c.c., driving by chain to the single rear wheel, which in its hub carried a two-speed epicyclic gear and clutch. Steering was by tiller. Although this machine was pretty elementary, its simplicity and solidity ensured its survival until 1915. The price (less comforts such as windshield, top, and apron) was always under £100 (then $500), and as early as 1910, a military version was made as a machine-gun carrier. Maximum speed was around 30 m.p.h.

56 VALVELESS 25 h.p., 1910, Great Britain

From 1901, a Cambridge engineer called Ralph Lucas built experimental two-stroke cars that he christened the Lucas Valveless. One type, of which three were made, had two pistons in the single cylinder. Others had two cylinders, with one piston in each, one crankshaft per cylinder, and a common combustion chamber. The centrally-mounted engine had transverse crankshafts, and the two-speed transmission was by dog clutches and chain. Although an epicyclic reverse gear was later provided, early cars could only proceed backwards by reversing the engine. In 1908, Lucas approached Thomas Cooper of the Cooper Steam Digger Company of King's Lynn (42) and asked him to build a run of fifty of his cars. But Lucas and Cooper fell out, so the former went to David Brown & Sons of Huddersfield for the construction of these machines. Called simply Valveless, they were more conventional, with crankshaft in a normal line (though transverse cylinders), a friction clutch, three-speed sliding-pinion gear-box, shaft drive, and bevel axle. The engine was now located forward, in the usual position. This first David Brown-built model of 1908 was called the 20 h.p.; then, for 1909–11, it was renamed the 25 h.p. though retaining the same engine dimensions. At this time it was supplemented by a new 15 h.p. The later 'big' Valveless used a smaller engine, a four-speed gear-box, and worm final drive.

57 BRUSH 10 h.p., 1910, U.S.A.

Alanson P. Brush, who had previously designed the first Cadillac, set up the Brush Runabout Company in Detroit in 1907, to make his own cars. These were 'gas-buggies' on the typical American lines of the period (up to a point); cheap, light in weight, powered by a big single-cylinder engine. The price at its lowest point was a mere $500 (then £100). The earliest cars had a 6 h.p. engine, and solid tires: the latter feature was soon dropped. The model shown is the 10 h.p., current in 1910 and 1911. It was fitted with pneumatic tires. The engine had a mechanically-operated inlet valve, and ignition was by coil and battery. Unlike most American runabouts of the period, this power unit could rev. up to 2,500 r.p.m., and was fitted with a crankshaft vibration damper. The Brush used not only wooden wheels and a wooden body, which was usual enough, but wooden axles as well. The recipe sounds flimsy, but in fact one of these cars was the first to cross Australia from west to east, in the hands of Francis Birtles in 1912. The 'outback' was even less kind to motor vehicles then than now, so the car must have been stronger than it looked. Suspension was by coil springs all round, which was also unconventional, but the final drive by chain was not; nor was the two-speed epicyclic transmission. The firm became part of the United States Motors group, and died with that combine in 1913.

58 BENZ 20/35 h.p., 1910, 1911, Germany

Karl Benz and Gottlieb Daimler have safe places in history as the men who made the gasoline-engined motor-car a practical proposition, and Benz can claim the further distinction of being the first to put it into commercial production, and to design it as an entity entirely independent of the horse-drawn carriage. But all this had happened by 1891. Technical progress caught up with Benz, who thought he had devised the perfect motor-car, and left him far behind. By 1902, when the original type was finally discontinued, the feeble, frail-looking, elementary Benz with its lazy horizontal engine, belt final drive, vestigial power output, and gentle 15–20 m.p.h. pace, which had been so popular up to 1900, was a museum piece. The firm took a long time to make up the lost ground (which meant catching up with Mercedes and Renault): the cars of the new designer, Marius Barbarou, formerly of Clement-Gladiator, were an advance on their predecessors, but were still too conservative to be competitive. However, in 1904, Barbarou (who went back to France, and Delaunay-Belleville) was replaced as works manager by Hans Nibel, who produced a line of splendidly made cars of conventional modern design, quite expensive, some medium-sized but owing their reputation to the big, fast cars in the range. All were fours until 1914, with pair-cast cylinders. The early Nibel cars had side valves in a T head, but he adopted the L-head layout in 1909. Shaft drive could be fitted to the 18/28 PS of 1905–8 as an option, but the largest machines could only be had with chain drive until 1908, and only in that year was a model offered with shaft drive alone, the 2·4-litre 10/18 PS, which was the 'baby'. The model shown is the 4·8-litre 20/35 h.p., which was current from 1909 to 1911, and was made in shaft-drive form only.

59 ADLER 7/15 PS, 1910, Germany

The Adler Fahrradwerke of Frankfurt was started by Heinrich Kleyer in 1886 to make bicycles. He later built motor-cycles too, and diversified further into aero engines and typewriters, for which the name is now known. Cars were made from 1899 to 1939. The first was, typically for Germany, a foreign-derived *voiturette*, in this case a shaft-driven, front-engined Renault-like vehicle with a De Dion engine in the latest idiom, and small cars were always the company's strong suit. Its 3½-h.p. engine was succeeded by the bigger 4½-h.p. De Dion unit, and then by the 6 h.p. and 8 h.p. Adler-built engines, one of them with two cylinders, that powered cars from 1902. By 1904 the single had gone, and twins carried on the *voiturette* tradition until 1909. However, in 1904 also, the first fours appeared; modern big cars with pair-cast cylinders, L heads, dual ignition, and (like every Adler) shaft drive. All these new machines, designed by Edmund Rumpler, were completely conventional, which could hardly be said for that which Rumpler laid out in 1903, with its all-round independent suspension by swing axles and unit construction of engine and gear-box; but this was not put into production. The 4/8 PS twin of 1906 combined the archaic feature of automatic inlet valves, dropped from other Adlers, with Rumpler's unit-construction engine and gear-box. The Adler fours gave birth to a line of very fierce sports cars, but the popular twins gave way in 1909 to the 6/14 PS small four, which was given a longer stroke in 1910 (100 mm.

instead of 88 mm.) to make 7/15 PS. This 1·8-litre car used the established layout of side valves in an L head, paired cylinders, dual ignition by magneto and coil, and three-speed unit gear-box. It was an extremely well made, reliable little machine.

60 STOEWER TYP B6, 1910, TYP C1, 1913, Germany

Emil and Bernhard Stoewer came into car manufacture conventionally enough, progressing from sewing-machines, typewriters, and bicycles to motor bicycles and tricycles in 1897; thence to a quadricycle. These were based on the De Dion Bouton from France, and were put together from parts supplied by Puteaux. A big rear-engined, chain-driven twin rather like an old-school Daimler followed. Still reflecting form, the company passed over to the *système* Panhard in 1901—an altogether more substantial theme, with two and four cylinders and chain drive—then to mechanically-operated inlet valves, steel frames, and the Mercedes model. From 1905 the *Gebrüder* Stoewer went modern, though remained conven-tional, with shaft drive, two, four, or six cylinders pair-cast, and valves in T-head formation. In 1906–7, L heads and then monobloc castings arrived on new models. The Typ B6 or 9/22 PS illustrated above, new in 1910, was also sold by another German firm, Mathis of Strasbourg, under the latter's name. The B6, although of only 2 litres' capacity, developed a reasonable 22 b.h.p. at 1,700 r.p.m. and could exceed 45 m.p.h. There were four forward speeds in a separate gear-box. The illustration below is of a Typ C1. By this time the *marque* was best known for small cars such as this (beginning with the 1910 Typ B1), though as in the case of Adler, who had a similar reputation (59), some sporting monsters were made as well.

61 PHÄNOMOBIL 4/6 PS, 1910, Germany

While the rest of Europe's motor industry in the first decade of the century was feeling its way towards the ultra-light car that would provide truly simple and economical motoring—a movement that produced the cyclecar —that of Germany, a nation that favoured big cars in this period, offered little of the nature of Britain's Riley, Jowett, or AC (44, 70, 55) or the tricars that preceded them in popular favour. The only popular analogies were the Piccolo (15), a four-wheeler, Karl Gustav Hiller's extraordinary three-wheeled Phänomobil, and the Cyklonette from which it was copied. The Phänomobil, made by the Phänomen Werke of Saxony from 1907 until as late as 1927, was very well liked for its economy of running and reliability, which overcame the drawbacks of a specification which sounds not merely highly unconventional, but lethal. The fan-cooled vee-twin engine was mounted on the forks of the single front wheel, and drove it by chain. The steering, which thus can hardly have inspired confidence, was controlled by tiller. The engine, which was quite exposed, punished the passengers with both noise and dirt. Transmission was by two-speed epicyclic gears. Various sizes of power unit were provided at different times, the car shown being the 4/6 PS of 1907–12, with 880 c.c., and in 1912 there was even a four-cylinder of $1\frac{1}{2}$ litres, which could be seen powering a miniature landaulet of bizarre appearance. These, at least, had mechanically-operated inlet valves; the twins used automatic inlet valves to the end. The Phänomen Werke had made bicycles and motor-cycles before turning to cars, and from 1911 offered a line of four-wheeled 'proper cars' as well, under the Phänomen name.

62 BIANCHI 20/30 h.p., 14/20 h.p., 1910, Italy

Edoardo Bianchi is said to have made a motor quadricycle as early as 1889, and his first true car followed in 1899. This was a *voiturette* with a single-cylinder of French De Dion origin, a tubular frame dating from Bianchi's interest in the bicycles which he had built since 1885, coil ignition and shaft drive. This little car made small impression even in Italy, but the same could not be said for the Giuseppe Merosi-designed Bianchis that followed in 1904. From then until 1909 they were big, well made, conventional machines with four pair-cast cylinders, side valves in a T head, low-tension magneto ignition, steel frames, honeycomb radiators, four forward speeds, and double-chain drive—in other words, they followed the Mercedes pattern closely. The 14/20 h.p. of 1909 witnessed a breakaway to a more modern design, with cylinders cast monobloc, an L-head valve layout, high-tension magneto ignition, and shaft drive. This is the model illustrated in the lower picture, in 1910 form. It was a 3-litre car, the smallest in the range, that had three forward speeds at first, then four. By 1911, all types except two $8\frac{1}{2}$- and $9\frac{1}{2}$-litre monsters, which retained pair-cast cylinders and chain drive, adhered to the new formula. The 20/30 h.p. shown above started life in 1909 with chain drive and a bi-bloc L-head engine of 4·9 litres' capacity, in which form it developed 25 b.h.p. at 1,250 r.p.m.; but in its later manifestation (1910–11) it fell into line with shaft drive and a monobloc engine, which had a longer stroke of 150 mm. providing 5·7 litres. It was capable in this form of rather over 50 m.p.h., and was completely typical of its breed. The car illustrated is an intermediate type, with shaft drive and pair-cast cylinders, dating from 1910.

63 MÉTALLURGIQUE
12 CV, 1910, 1911, Belgium

L'Auto Métallurgique S.A., makers of one of the superbly-engineered, refined, modern, fast, expensive machines for which Belgium was so famous until the late 1920s, started life in a much humbler manner, with their twin-cylinder and four-cylinder small cars of 1900 on Panhard or Daimler lines (with chain drive). They moved over to shaft drive and a live axle in 1902, and never departed from this layout henceforth. 1903 saw the arrival of Ernst Lehmann as designer, and 1905 the coming of the first Métallurgiques of the type which was going to be re-

nowned. Their shaft drive apart, they were built on Mercedes lines (which is not surprising, since Lehmann came from Daimler), with steel frames, honeycomb radiators, and T-head four-cylinder engines with variable valve lift. These cars had flat radiators, but in 1907, the more familiar acute vee made its bow. 1908 brought monobloc engines, and 1911, four-speed gear-boxes on all models. These were comparatively rare on any Belgian cars at the time, and no Métallurgiques had had them until three years before. Side valves in an L head were used except in the sporting versions of the touring cars, which had overhead inlet valves. The car shown was the smallest of the range in the last pre-war years, the 12 CV of 2·6 litres, which provided 32 b.h.p. (By this time there were only fours in the catalogue: the last twin had gone, and there was never a six.) The 12 CV was made from 1909 to 1914, and was very popular.

64 LE ZÈBRE 4 CV, 1911,
France

The S.A. Le Zèbre catered for the big French market for *voiturettes* with one of the tiniest of the breed. Introduced late in 1909, this Type A was a cheap and simple machine that weighed only $5\frac{1}{2}$ cwt. with a single-cylinder 4 CV engine of 600 c.c. The bore was enlarged by 3 mm. to 88 mm. in 1912, but otherwise the car remained unchanged until 1914. A 1911 model is illustrated. In many ways, it had points in common with full-scale cars—its plate clutch, three-speed sliding-pinion gear-box (from 1913: the first cars had two speeds), shaft drive to a live axle, and half-elliptic suspension were by no means general on bigger *voiturettes*. A minute L-head monobloc four joined it in 1912. This Type C's claim to fame is that it was the ancestor of the post-war 5 CV Citroen, which it resembled in not a few respects, not least in sharing the same designer, Salomon.

65 TURCAT-MÉRY 18 CV, 1911, France

Léon Turcat and Simon Méry, who were brothers-in-law, built their first car in Marseilles in 1898, and within a year they were on a production basis. These machines were of the German four-cylinder Daimler type except that the first model had coil and battery ignition, and were of excellent quality. In 1902 Baron de Turckheim of De Dietrich et Cie saved the Marseillaise firm by taking out a licence and giving Turcat and Méry jobs, but the latter went on making cars under their own names, independently. All models until 1908 retained chain drive, but from 1909, all were shaft-driven. Until 1913, they were fours with a stroke of 130 mm., and varying bores. They were conventional, well-built machines with a fine reputation, expensive, and made in small numbers. The 18 CV shown was one of the new 1909 range, with 3·3 litres. Beside it were a 14 CV, and (from 1910 to 1913) a bigger 25 CV. All had side valves in an L head, magneto ignition, a cone clutch, and four forward speeds. More powerful engines, including one of 40 CV, were installed in this chassis for competition

work. One of these 18/40 CV cars won the first Monte Carlo Rally in 1911, driven by Rougier.

66 CLÉMENT-BAYARD TYPE 4M, 1911, 1912, France

In 1903 Adolphe Clément, whose Clément-Gladiator Company had made his name in the motor world from 1898 with popular small cars, left the concern he had founded and set up on his own again, the new company being called the S.A. des Etablissements Clément-Bayard. The Chevalier Bayard, the *chevalier sans peur et sans reproche*, had been a French national hero since early in the sixteenth century. The first small Clément-Bayards were virtually iden-tical with his previous cars; and indeed, as late as 1907 some of his vehicles were said to differ from Gladiators (as his former products were called, now made by the Société Gladiator) only in having shaft drive. However, from then on, Clément, who had made some very big cars in his time, became known for small and medium-sized machines, all of excellent quality and very up-to-date design. The same year saw the intro-duction of a 1·6-litre L-head monobloc four with unit construction of engine and gear-box, very early days for such a modern layout. Also in 1907, another feature of the make henceforth to be familiar appeared; a dashboard radiator. By the time the car shown was made, the standard small four was the 8 CV Type 4 M, of 1·3 litres. This car achieved a reputation as one of the best of its type on the French market.

67 ROCHET-SCHNEIDER 25 CV, 1911, France

The Etablissements Rochet-Schneider was one of many Lyons firms offering solid, durable, well made, unexciting motor-cars for the middle classes. After starting life with belt-drive *voiturettes*, they went over first to the Panhard system and then to the Mercedes, when each in turn became the criterion for more expensive cars. They had no new ideas of their own. The 20/22 h.p. of 1903, a car of Mercedes type except for its frame of armoured wood instead of channel steel, was the machine that began to make the name; and it must have had something, since the design was made under licence in several countries—by Moyea and Sampson in the United States, Nagant and FN in Belgium, Florentia in Italy, and Martini in Switzerland. In the latter incarnation, it won more publicity than under its original name, thanks to the publicity efforts of Captain H. H. P. Deasy in Britain, who launched the new car with an ascent of the Rochers de Naye cogwheel railway in Switzerland. These early Mercedes-type Rochet-Schneiders had, of course, four-cylinder side-valve T-head engines, low-tension ignition, a four-speed gate-change gear-box, and double-chain drive. By the time the car shown was made, in 1911, L-head engines with high-tension ignition and shaft drive had arrived. The machine illustrated is the four-cylinder 4·8-litre 25 CV current from 1911 to 1913; the largest of the fours (though there was also a 5½-litre six). The later cars had monobloc engines. Unlike many manufacturers of pedestrian vehicles, Rochet-Schneider never raced.

68 WOLSELEY 16/20 h.p., 1911, 1912, Great Britain

It was usual around the turn of the century to find bicycle manufacturers turning to cars, and not even makers of sewing-machines and typewriters were uncommon, all being precision machines, but the make under discussion was probably unique in its origins in the Wolseley Sheep Shearing Machine Company. Herbert Austin made his first car for them in 1896; a copy of the French Léon Bollée tricar. However, his four-wheeled prototype of 1899, with slow-turning horizontal engine at the front and chain final drive, formed the basis of the Wolseley up to 1906, save for the substitution of chain for belt primary drive in the production cars. The 10-h.p. (later 12-h.p.) twin was the most popular. These cars were well liked for their qualities of extremely strong construction, reliability and simplicity, which outweighed the increasingly backward design. When in 1905 the company decided to follow fashion and make cars with vertical engines and shaft drive, to the design of J. D. Siddeley (one of the directors), Austin departed, although he was to build the same kind of machine under his own name (44, 69). The new type went by the name of Wolseley-Siddeley, until Siddeley's departure in 1909 to take over the Deasy concern (54) caused a reversion to the original name a year later. The Wolseley was by then an orthodox, beautifully made machine of medium to large size, with four or six pair-cast cylinders, high-tension magneto ignition, side valves in a T head, four forward speeds, and shaft drive. Only the worm final drive was at all unusual. The 16/20 h.p. of 1911 and 1912, shown here, was of 3·1 litres. It was made from 1910 to 1915, and was the best-seller of its range.

69 AUSTIN 15 h.p., 1911, Great Britain

In 1911, when the car illustrated was built, it was representative of the type of machine for which Herbert Austin was by then well known: the high-quality, medium-sized, four-cylinder machine of completely conventional specification but considerable refinement. At this date most of his models were technically rather old-fashioned, with their separately cast cylinders and T-head configuration, but all had shaft drive. The 15 h.p. actually retrogressed, having started life in 1908–10 with a monobloc engine. The luxury of dual ignition (high-tension magneto and coil and battery) was provided as standard on all models except the 7 h.p. (45) and all from 1909 had four forward speeds. The modern 15 h.p., introduced in 1909, had an engine of 2·8 litres, and was the smallest model in the catalogue until the advent of the 10-h.p. light car in 1911, which was another up-to-date design. It was a lively machine, especially when fitted with light two-passenger bodies like that shown, but it was also seen in town-car guise with underfloor engine and no hood.

70 JOWETT, 1911(?), Great Britain

Benjamin and William Jowett made engines—for stationary use, and for supplying to car manufacturers—before they built complete cars, but from 1910 (or, some say, 1913) until 1953 (an extraordinarily long run for a single basic design) they offered vehicles powered by their famous flat-twin power unit, which was exceptionally rugged. From the beginning until 1939, the engine was at the heart of one of the best small cars of its day. What are said to be 1911 examples of the earliest production version are illustrated here, with its unit construction of 826 c.c., water-cooled engine and three-speed gear-box, and shaft drive to a worm-geared rear axle that was furnished with a differential. In a number of ways, the Jowett was considerably in advance of its time, even though it was steered by tiller and not wheel. Indeed, a prototype was built as early as 1906. The first production cars weighed only $6\frac{1}{2}$ cwt., and since the engine, though tiny, had excellent low-speed torque, they performed very well. However, they were best known for the uncomplaining longevity of their engines. Wheel steering came in 1914, and a bevel drive and a bigger engine shortly thereafter.

71 ARROL-JOHNSTON 15.9 h.p., 1911, Great Britain

Like the Albion (13), the Arrol-Johnston was from its beginnings an uncompromisingly solid, simple machine in which strength, reliability and longevity, vital qualities on the Scottish roads of the day, were the paramount virtues. Fashion was one of the other considerations disregarded in the early cars, which from 1900 to

1905 were seen with one- or two-cylinder opposed-piston engines turning at only 800 r.p.m., low-tension flywheel magneto ignition, high wheels, solid tires, and a towering dogcart body that was outdated when it was first fitted. In 1905, a more modern concept with front engine and shaft instead of chain drive appeared alongside the primeval dogcart. This 18 h.p. retained a twin-cylinder opposed-piston engine, and others of the type followed: a 12 h.p., and a three-cylinder in two sizes, both with unit-construction gearboxes. Not until 1907 did conventional cars enter the range—two overhead-inlet-valve fours. Although the makers entered the Tourist Trophy Race three times (in 1905 when they won, in 1906, and in 1907), and in 1908 a special air-cooled car went to Antarctica with Ernest Shackleton, such publicity was not enough to overcome public prejudice against unconventional design. Arrol-Johnston became a widely-known name only after T. C. Pullinger became Managing Director in 1909. He concentrated on combining the classic virtues of the make with generally unadventurous but thoroughly modern design. His first new model, out late in 1909, is shown here in 1911 form—the 15·9 h.p. This had four cylinders totalling 2·4 litres and a side-valve L-head layout, high-tension magneto ignition, shaft drive, and rear full-elliptic springs. The car stood out from most of its class because of its detachable wheels and dashboard radiator, and in 1909–11 could be had with Allen-Liversedge front-wheel brakes. These were not very efficient, and were soon dropped. Otherwise, the 15·9 h.p. was the epitome of the

typical well made, middle-sized, middle-class car.

72 AMERICAN UNDERSLUNG 50 h.p., 1911, U.S.A.

In 1907 Harry C. Stutz (later to be famous for the sporting car bearing his own name) designed a remarkable machine for the American Motor Car Company of Indianapolis, that was to be current until 1914. For two years previously, the company had made a normal car, but the new one was of note because of its extremely low centre of gravity, obtained by underslinging the chassis frame below the axles at front and rear. At the same time, there was a good ground clearance (of 11 inches), so necessary on American roads at the time. The rest of this big, powerful, fast and expensive machine was conventional enough, seen here in 1911 form with its Teetor-Hartley-built, four-cylinder side-valve T-head engine, of 50 h.p., 8·2 litres, and almost 'square' dimensions, dual ignition, four-speed gear-box and shaft drive. This particular model was current from 1908 to 1913. There was also, from 1914, an even bigger six-cylinder 70 h.p. chassis. Four- or two-passenger bodies could be had.

73 FRANKLIN MODEL D, 1911, U.S.A.

The H. H. Franklin Manufacturing Company was remarkable in that it never offered anything but cars with air-cooled engines, and from the beginning (in 1902) they had at least four cylinders. The latter feature was highly unusual in what was otherwise a typical 'gas-buggy' of the time, light and small, with its two-speed epicyclic gears and single-chain drive. Further, this engine used mechanically-operated overhead exhaust valves, with pushrods that passed through the exhaust downpipes. This type was continued until 1906, by which time it had bigger company: the six of 1905, which was a full-sized car with a 30-h.p. engine of more conventional design (all-overhead valves, pushrod-operated), shaft drive, and a three-speed sliding-pinion gearbox. The cylinders were separately cast, as before, but they were in a fore-and-aft line instead of transversely mounted. There was a round hood, in the fashion set by Delaunay-Belleville and Hotchkiss in France (52, 53). A similar four was beside it. By 1911, the hood had been changed to the Renault type that was to be a Franklin 'trademark', and is shown in the illustrations, which are of the Model D of that year. This was a six-cylinder development of the four-cylinder Model D that had been in the range since 1909. It had a cubic capacity of five litres, and an 'over-square' engine. The Model D was current until 1913 but it retained one of the peculiarities of the very first cars: their full-elliptic suspension. The Franklin proved itself in many gruelling dry-weather tests, including two record-breaking crossings of the United States, in 1904 and 1905, and repeated success in the Los Angeles–Phoenix desert races of 1908–15. Clearly another idiosyncrasy, the reinforced wooden frame, did not imply weakness either.

74 BUICK 24/30 h.p.
BEDFORD-BUICK
15/18 h.p., 1911, U.S.A.

David Dunbar Buick was a maker of plumbers' fittings and furnishings before he turned to cars. An experimental vehicle was built in 1900. This was followed by engines, and in 1904 by the first production car. Only a few were made, but a year later the Buick Motor Company received an infusion of new capital from William Crapo Durant. Under Durant production increased twenty times over, at first on the basis of the two-cylinder car. This was a 22-h.p. flat twin with epicyclic gears, chain final drive and the unusual feature of all-overhead valves (which were, however, exposed). Buick left in 1906, and in the same year the first Buick with four vertical cylinders arrived; the 30-h.p. Model D, which was a full-sized shaft-driven machine. The twin continued. Both cars retained the two-speed epicyclic transmission, as did the 15/20 h.p. of 1908. The latter's engine had 'square' dimensions of 95 × 95 mm., giving 2·7 litres, and there was dual ignition by coil and magneto. There was also a 24/30 h.p. of $4\frac{1}{2}$ litres (top illustration). In the same year Buick became the nucleus of Durant's General Motors Company, which in 1909 founded a subsidiary, the Bedford Motor Company, in London to sell British-assembled Buicks in Britain. Three of these were offered as the Bedford-Buick or Bedford, one of which was the 15/18 h.p. illustrated (bottom), which was the American 15/20 h.p. The model first introduced to Britain, the last named, was also the longest lived, being the only survivor in 1914. It was well built and reliable. Its only serious modification was the introduction of a sliding-pinion three-speed gear-box in all models in place of epicyclic gearing late in 1911, following a similar change in the American design.

75 CHEVROLET MODEL C, 1911, CLASSIC SIX, 1912, U.S.A.

Louis Chevrolet was one of the legion of Swiss engineers who left his own country, which did not encourage the growth of an automobile industry, to give his talents to foreign countries. (Others were Ernest Henry of Peugeot, Marc Birkigt of Hispano-Suiza, and Georges Roesch of Talbot.) He sold the De Dion Bouton (16) in America, and raced other makes, including Buick. He also made his own car as early as 1909, but also designed a six for William Crapo Durant, of whose General Motors Company Buick formed a part (74). However, the six-cylinder car, which Durant launched at the end of 1911, bore its designer's name. The machine illustrated at the top of the page is one of the original Model C Chevrolets, of which five prototypes were made in 1911, while the other is one of the Chevrolet Motor Company's first production models of 1912; the Classic Six. Three thousand were built in the first year. It was the company's staple until 1914, when the much cheaper, smaller four-cylinder overhead valve Baby Grand touring and Royal Mail roadster were introduced. It was, in fact, a $2,500 middle-class car built to Chevrolet's own exacting standards, which were not those of his employer. He left Durant at the end of 1913 to found the Frontenac Motor Company. The side-valve, T-head engine, made by the Mason Motor Company, had cylinders cast in threes and a cubic capacity of nearly 5 litres, and the wheelbase was an impressive 10 feet. Power output was 50 b.h.p., which was required to pull 31 cwt. of open touring car. A compressed-air self-starter was fitted as standard.

76 STANLEY 10 h.p., 1911, U.S.A.

Francis E. and Freelan O. Stanley made and sold a light steam car in small numbers from 1897, but sold their rights in it two years later to the Locomobile Company of America, who made a great success of it under their own name. The Locomobile steamer was built until 1904, but the Stanley brothers were able to restart car manufacture after 1902 by the terms of their agreement, and did so. The result was an altogether bigger and stronger machine. The basic design was similar, power being provided by a simple horizontal two-cylinder double-acting engine, except that the new design used a kerosene instead of a gasoline burner, and had longitudinal front suspension instead of transverse. Cars with three sizes of engine were sold from 1905–6: the 10-h.p. Model E (lever EX), and the 20-h.p. Model F later (from 1907) available enlarged as the 30-h.p. Model K. Maximum speed of the 10 h.p. with the standard touring body shown was rather over 30 m.p.h., though 50 m.p.h. was available for short bursts. Versions prepared for racing in British speed events could reach between 60 and 70 m.p.h. This range remained fundamentally unchanged until 1913, only the type designation changing, and the size of the 10-h.p. engine going up slightly. By 1911 type designations had changed: the four-passenger 10 h.p. was called the Type 63. The 10 h.p. was dropped for 1914.

77 OPEL 6/16 PS, 1911, Germany

By 1909, Opel had established themselves as Germany's foremost constructors of well built, modestly priced, small cars of modern design. These were the company's strength, and in that year consisted entirely of fours; the 4/8 PS (50), the 6/14 PS and the 8/16 PS, of between 1·1 and 1·8 litres. Two new models arrived in 1910; the short-lived 1,200-c.c. 5/10 PS (5/11 PS for 1911), and the 1,540-c.c. 6/16 PS illustrated, which was developed from the 6/14 PS. The 6/16 PS proved a very popular car, that remained current until 1914. Its L-head monobloc engine developed 16 b.h.p. at 1,750 r.p.m., and unlike the 5/10 PS and the earlier small fours, it had four forward speeds. Like all of them, however, it was a completely conventional car with its magneto ignition, cone clutch, separate gear-box and half-elliptic suspension front and rear. Top speed was around 40 m.p.h. Still more famous was the replacement for the 5/11 PS that arrived in 1912, and was made until 1914: the 5/14 PS 'Puppchen', or 'Doll', of 1·4 litres, that also had a four-speed gear-box like its bigger brother. This car and the 6/16

PS made Opel Germany's biggest producer. The thousandth Opel was made in 1908; by 1912, 10,000 had been built.

78 GRÄF UND STIFT 18/32 PS, 1911, Austria

Karl, Franz, and Heinrich Gräf were brothers who set themselves up in bicycle manufacture in Vienna in 1896. The first Gräf car dated from 1897; it was unusual in that its De Dion-type engine drove the front wheels. Production was planned in 1899, but did not begin at once. From 1902 conventional cars were made for the motor dealer Arnold Spitz, under his own name. Wilhelm Stift provided finance in 1902, and after 1907, where the Spitz connection ended, the machines were called Gräf und Stift. The firm became known for conservative, beautifully built vehicles that gained a reputation for quality second to none among Austrian constructors. All were fours, with T-head bi-bloc engines varying in size from 4·2 to 10 litres, four forward speeds, and shaft drive. The car shown is the 18/32 PS of 1911, offering a mere 32 b.h.p. at 1,400 r.p.m. from 5·8 litres. Maximum speed was rather over 50 m.p.h. In this particular machine, the Archduke Franz Ferdinand and his wife were murdered at Sarajevo in 1914. It is preserved in Vienna and still shows the bullet holes.

79 FN TYPE 1560, TYPE 1600, 1911, Belgium

The FN (its initials standing for

Fabrique Nationale d'Armes de Guerre) was Belgium's only make that was best known for low-priced, straightforward cars made in considerable quantities for a middle-class market. They were of excellent quality, too, sharing this feature but none of the others with the rest of Belgium's motor industry, which concentrated (to its cost) upon fairly conventional but very expensive, large, fast machinery made in small numbers for the wealthy. Characteristically, no fewer than 100 of the first FN models were built in the first full year of manufacture, 1900. It was a twin-cylinder *voiturette* with two speeds and chain final drive. In 1902, a four-cylinder car with shaft drive was offered; then nothing new (and, for a while, no cars at all) until the arrival in 1906 of a big chain-driven machine built under Rochet-Schneider licence. This was a bi-bloc side-valve T-head affair, but later the same year, a more modern L-head, shaft-driven car appeared. It formed the basis of the very popular 2-litre Type 2000 of 1908 and its developments. By 1908, three or four FNs were being turned out every day. There was a smaller four, the 70 × 90 mm. 1400, which by the time of the 1909 Paris Salon had developed into the 1500, with a foot throttle and a stronger frame. The same car, with a bigger bore than the 1560 and shown here in 1911 guise, is illustrated above a further development of the small-car theme, the 1600 new in the same year. This car was distinguished by a four-speed gear-box, and a rear fuel tank. The 200, with the other models in the range, acquired a monobloc engine in 1912, but that was the last year of the smaller car.

80 SCANIA 18/20 h.p., 18/24 h.p., 1911, Sweden

The Maskin A.B. Scania of Malmo, who had made the Humber bicycle from Britain under licence since 1894, never built cars in more than small series. Until 1902 they were assembled machines with German-built Kämper engines at rear or front, at first designed by Fridolf Thorssin and then by Anton Svenson. A run of six of the latter were made; the company's first excursion into series production. In the same year their first Swedish design arrived; a 6-h.p. air-cooled vertical twin. Varying patterns were still being tried in 1903— a 6 h.p. with water cooling, and two of 8 h.p.: one type with coil ignition, two forward speeds and an underslung radiator, and another, more modern, with magneto ignition, three speeds, and radiator before engine. There was an overhead-valve engine with wet cylinder liners in 1905. From 1910, only Scania-made engines were fitted. These came, over the years, in considerable variety, ranging from singles through twins to fours, yet between 1908 and 1912, only a few dozen Scanias were built in all. In 1911, the year of the cars shown, the firm amalgamated with the Vagnfabriks A. B. i. Sodertalje, who had also made cars in penny packets but were more interested in commercial vehicles, to form the A. B. Scania-Vabis. Scanias continued to be made under their own name by the new firm into 1912, and the Vabis until 1915. From 1914, cars called Scania-Vabis began to make their appearance. The range offered in 1911 consisted of 15, 18/20 and 18/24 h.p. models. All were fours with side-valve engines and shaft drive (except the largest, 45/60 h.p. which was available with shaft or chain drive). The car shown above is a 2·3-litre 18/20 h.p. of 1911, with curiously conservative bodywork for the year. The other machine, also of 1911, is less elegant but more modern, with the fashionable flush-sided coachwork. It is an 18/24 h.p. of 2·5 litres. The 18/20 h.p. and 18/24 h.p. were still listed in 1912, but as before, they were actually made only in minute numbers.

81 BERLIET 12 CV, 1912, France

In 1895 Marius Berliet, with the backing of Emile Lavirotte (who had already made his own car, the Audibert-Lavirotte), started manufacture in Lyons with three employees in the Lavirotte works. Thus modestly began one of the notable names (which still exists) in the motor industry of that city (second only to that of Paris, and second to none in the production of high-quality, expensive cars). At first, like so many other manufacturers, Berliet made *voiturettes*, which in 1900 boasted unit construction of engine and gear-box. Later Berliets were very orthodox machines, however. The first fours, Panhard-like machines, appeared in 1901, and thereafter the development of design was largely predictable. The 1902 Paris Salon saw the adoption in part of the *système* Mercedes, with a 24-h.p. chain-driven T-head four. The first shaft-driven car came in 1907, and the first six two seasons later. The former, a 15 CV, became Berliet's most popular pre-1914 model, and is shown here in 12 CV, 1912 guise. The engine

was a four-cylinder, 2·4-litre unit with side valves in an L head, and magneto ignition. The cylinders could be had pair-cast or monobloc. There were four forward speeds, in a separate gear-box. The 12 CV was current until 1915. Interestingly, Berliet experimented with superchargers from 1905, and in 1908 a supercharged model was listed in the catalogue. From 1905 to 1913, Berliets were made under licence in the United States under the name of Alco (American Locomotive Company). They won the 1909 and 1910 Vanderbilt Cup Races. Berliet, a sedate concern, did little competition work in Europe: they chalked up one important win only, in the Targa Bologna Race of 1908.

82 PANHARD-LEVASSOR 15 CV, 1912, France

In 1891, Emile Levassor had been responsible for the design of a machine that was to set the basic theme of the motor-car for the next two generations: after experimenting with a rear- and centre-mounted engine such as earlier cars had, he put the power unit at the front and drove the rear wheels via a friction clutch and sliding-pinion gears. In 1898, the firm pioneered pneumatic tires on production cars, self-centring steering, and a steering wheel on a raked column. After this, design stagnated at Ivry-Port; the make became a byword for conservatism, fine materials and workmanship, straightforward design, solidity, and reliability. After providing the great example, Panhard et Levassor, like most other people, became copiers; in their case of Mercedes, who were now the arbiters of fashion among makers of more expensive cars. Even so, the conversion did not come until 1904, and was then only partial. As late as 1902, hot-tube ignition was optional, pressed-steel frames did not come until 1905, and a gate change did not finally oust the quadrant until 1910. Conventionally, there were as many as nine models in the 1909 range, the smaller with shaft drive, the rest chain-driven, one of them a vast 11-litre 65-h.p. six with pair-cast cylinders that had all the vices of most early examples of the breed, summed up in general noise and lack of refinement (the drawbacks the layout was designed to mitigate). Not even Panhard's partial conversion to Charles Yale Knight's double sleeve-valve engine in 1910 was very daring; Daimler of Coventry, an equally tradition-bound concern, had anticipated them by two years, and so had Minerva of Belgium. The car illustrated is a 15 CV of 1912; this 2·6-litre machine was the smaller of two sleeve-valve cars available, the other being the 20 CV of 1910–13. The cylinders were cast in pairs, though the bigger cars had separately cast cylinders; and chain drive was still obtainable to choice, though the vehicle shown has shaft drive. It was designated the X17 in 1912, and the X21 from 1913 up to its demise in 1916. An extraordinary relic of Panhard conservatism was the armoured-wood frame, retained by the car illustrated.

83 H.L. 10/15 CV, 12/18 CV, 1912, France

Messrs. Hainsselin and Langlois of Saint-Cloud made cars of original design from 1912 to 1914; a time when most manufacturers large and small were rapidly losing the eccentricities of earlier days. The chassis was unorthodox in that it had independent front suspension by sliding pillars and coil springs. The engine itself was normal— either a 10/15 CV or a 12/18 CV, of 2·4 and 3 litres respectively, both with side valves—but it was installed in a very light and spindly frame. Since the engines turned at a respectable 2,400 r.p.m., and complete cars without bodies weighed around 9 cwt., the power-to-weight ration was very good and the maximum speed was nearly 60 and nearly 70 m.p.h. in each case, but as the brakes were notably poor, it is hard to see this performance being usable. One of each type made is illustrated. Furthermore, there was no conventional gear-box: instead, a two-speed rear axle.

84 SCHNEIDER TH. 18 CV, 1912, France

Automobiles Th. Schneider of Besançon started life in 1910, at the instance of Théophile Schneider, who had earlier helped to found the Rochet–Schneider company (67). His cars were all normal, modern, side-valve L-head fours or sixes with shaft drive and the common feature of a dashboard radiator. The first one was a 1·7-litre 12 CV. In 1911 there were six types, from a 10 CV of 1·8 litres to a big 5-litre 25 CV. In that year, too, monobloc engines were introduced, and the company's only pre-1914 six, a 15 CV, made its brief appearance. The car shown is an 18 CV of 1912. The firm's racing machines took part in most of the important competitions of 1912–14, but without success: they were no doubt too 'touring' in their antecedents to compete with the sophisticated Grand Prix cars of the time. One machine entered in the 1912 French Grand Prix probably had a sleeve-valve engine, but though it departed in this from the contemporary touring cars, which had poppet valves, the innovation was not one to stir the blood.

85 BELSIZE 10/12 h.p., 1912, Great Britain

Like practically all British cars at the time, the Marshall of 1897–1903 was of foreign origin; it was unusual only in that it had two ancestors instead of one. It was derived from the Hurtu from France, which in turn was a copy of the German Benz, a retrograde design by this time. The Belsize Motor & Engineering Company that succeeded Marshall & Company was more imaginative; their 12-h.p. shaft-driven three-cylinder of 1901 was a modern machine with an engine made by the Société Buchet of Paris that was regarded as very efficient, not only because of its mechanically-operated inlet valves, but also because of its good 'breathing' and high compression ratio for the day, all of which made for high revolutions. Belsize developed the Buchet engine themselves and gained a name for efficiency. The most popular Belsizes were the smaller ones, of which the 10/12 h.p. of 1912 is shown. Outwardly conventional with its four-cylinder side-valve engine, it concealed also unit construction of engine and gear-box and worm final drive.

86 ROVER TWELVE, 1912, Great Britain

From 1904 until 1912, the Rover Company made their name in the car world (having already done so with bicycles) with excellent single-cylinder *voiturettes* of 6 h.p. and 8 h.p. These were well-made, strong, and reliable; but their designer, E. W. Lewis, added a 16/20-h.p. four in 1905. This and the succeeding model, the 20 h.p., were sound cars, even if the ball-bearing crankshaft was noisy. One of them won the 1907 Tourist Trophy Race. Several lesser known machines followed, before Owen Clegg, formerly of Wolseley, arrived in 1911 together with other Wolseley personnel. His Twelve, illustrated, was a conventional but thoroughly modern and good car in all respects, once transmission failures were overcome, winning an enviable reputation in the middle-class market with their Rover virtues. Where sanctions of a dozen cars had been commonplace before, 500 of the Twelve were put in hand at a time. By 1914, it was alone in the Rover range. It was powered by a 2·3-litre L-head monobloc engine with four cylinders. Final drive was by worm. The model was continued until 1924, being renamed the Fourteen towards the end of its life. Clegg went on to design the equally good 16 h.p. Darracq of 1913, which bore a close family resemblance to the Rover.

87 IRIS 15 h.p., 1912, Great Britain

The Iris car was put together carefully, in small numbers, by Legros & Knowles

Ltd. of London between late 1904 and around 1914. The 1904 cars, a 25 h.p. and a 35 h.p., were almost entirely conventional machines, their only peculiarity being coil ignition, the lack of a fourth forward speed, and the highly attractive diamond-shaped radiator. At the same time the specifications were up to date, incorporating shaft drive, save on the first few cars which were chain-driven, and an L-head engine with a short stroke. The four cylinders were pair-cast. A six-cylinder car on similar lines arrived in 1906. Legros & Knowles went into receivership in 1908, but the firm was reborn the following year, as Iris Cars Ltd. At its head was G. A. Mower, an American, who in 1910 introduced a new model, the 15 h.p. illustrated in 1912 form, alongside the older types. This 2·3-litre car was a modern design, with L-head monobloc engine and high-tension magneto ignition, but still only a three-speed gear-box. It was endowed with a ball-bearing crankshaft in 1911. The larger, by now antediluvian models continued alongside it to the end.

88 SUNBEAM 12/16 h.p.,
1912, Great Britain

After an odd excursion producing what was probably the most eccentric machine successfully offered to the credulous public in the early days of motoring, the Sunbeam-Mabley, John Marston of Wolverhampton, makers of the fine Sunbeam bicycle, engaged T. C. Pullinger to make proper motor-cars. Sensibly, Pullinger went to the Berliet from France for inspiration for his first, 1902 car: a chain-driven four with automatic inlet valves of Panhard type and normal and proven specification. Another Berliet type succeeded it in 1905, now with mechanically-operated inlet valves. Pullinger left to go to Humber when the Sunbeam Motor Car Company was formed that year, and design devolved upon Angus Shaw. His new, non-Berliet 16/20 h.p. of 1906 had an L-head engine, as did the six-cylinder but otherwise identical 25/30 h.p. of 1907 and its successor the 1908 35 h.p., but they retained the archaic armoured-wood frame, had separately cast cylinders, were quite uninspired designs, and sold badly. All was changed when the Breton Louis Coatalen replaced Shaw in 1908. From being a little-known maker of conservative cars, Sunbeam became famous in three or four years. This was partly thanks to Coatalen's new design, which was conventional, yet very modern and highly efficient. His 14/20 h.p. of 1909 still had pair-cast cylinders, but the long-stroke 3·8-litre T-head unit (later called the 16/20 h.p.) developed no less than 54 b.h.p., thanks to an ability to turn at 2,300 r.p.m. At first, buyers could have either chain or shaft drive. The basically similar 2·4-litre 12/16 h.p. (shown here in 1912 form), which was available only with shaft drive, arrived later the same year, and the third basic model, the six-cylinder 25/30 h.p. on the same general lines, came in 1911. That year's models only had worm final drive. The 12/16's pair-cast cylinders gave way to an L-head monobloc layout in 1912, when a longer stroke of 150 mm. was provided too, giving just over three litres. The model was current until 1914 as the 12/16 h.p. Rover made it during the war, and Sunbeam continued it after the war in almost identical form until 1921. By 1911 the name of Sunbeam was beginning to be celebrated not only for the excellence of its products, but also for racing successes on Brooklands Motor Course, with very special racing cars. Greater fame came when in 1911, 1912, and 1913, racing machines that were fundamentally similar to the production touring cars entered in the Coupé de l'Auto Race, winning in 1912 and coming third in 1913, and, entered in the concurrent French Grand Prix, took third place in both years against much more advanced opposition. The 1911 and 1912 Coupé de l'Auto cars were based on the 12/16 h.p. and in 1912 form produced 87 b.h.p. at 3,000 r.p.m. Their success led to the marketing of a mildly-tuned sports version of the racers; a fast and pretty car that was made in small numbers. A 1911 25/30 h.p. was third in the Indianapolis 500 Miles Race of 1913. One of the 1913 Grand Prix cars was seventh in 1914. A very special twin-overhead-camshaft 16-valve racing car based on the 1913 Peugeots won the Tourist Trophy in 1914. Company profits rose from £90 ($450) in 1909 to more than a thousand times that figure four years later, thanks to Coatalen's efforts.

89 **MORRIS-OXFORD,**
1913, Great Britain

Like so many in his generation, William Richard Morris was in the bicycle and motor-cycle trade before he made cars—he repaired, sold, and built two-wheelers, his first motor-cycle seeing the light of day in 1903. Then he started hiring and trading in cars, and from 1910 planned one of his own. It was announced in October 1912, and a prototype (less engine) was exhibited in February 1913. Although none was sold until April 1913, it is included in this book because it is an early British example of a type very soon to open up a vast new market in Europe: the light car, or big car in miniature. When the new car appeared it was christened the Morris-Oxford, after the city on the outskirts of which it was built. 1,475 of this first Morris, which is illustrated here, were built up to the end of production in 1917. It was an assembled machine of the most modern type. It was reliable, long-lived, strong, and had a very useful performance (maximum speed was around 50 m.p.h.). The monobloc engine of this first Oxford was smooth and flexible. It was made by White & Poppe, in unit with a three-speed gear-box, and the worm final drive was by Wrigley. Unusually at so late a date, the valves were in a T-head arrangement. The price in 1913 was £173 ($865) for the standard two-passenger model, and a year later forty a week were being turned out. Weight was 12½ cwt. When Morris sought a more powerful engine for a four-passenger car that had still to sell at a low price, he went to Continental of Detroit, and the 1½-litre Cowley of 1915 was the outcome.

90 **K.R.I.T. 25/30 h.p.**, 1912, U.S.A.

The K.R.I.T. was made by Kenneth Krittenden of Detroit from 1909 to 1916. It was at all times an orthodox machine in most respects. Deviations from the norm visible on the model illustrated, the 25/30 h.p. of 1912, were confined to full-elliptic rear springs. Otherwise, there was a four-cylinder side-valve monobloc engine of 2·9 litres, magneto ignition, three-speed gear-box, and shaft drive to a live axle. This 25/30 h.p. was current from 1911 to 1913; a modest machine trying to compete in the low-priced market against giants such as Buick (74), Maxwell (47), and Reo, with predictable results.

91 RAMBLER 38 h.p., 1912, U.S.A.

Thomas B. Jeffery started the Rambler car business from bicycle-manufacturing beginnings. Various prototypes appeared between 1897 and 1902, and in the latter year came the first production car, the Model C, which was characteristic of its period and country in being a lightweight with big, slow-turning single-cylinder engine. It was more modern than most of its breed in having a mechanically-operated inlet valve, and it was very popular, taking second place after Oldsmobile in numbers produced in 1902. Like other American 'gas buggies', the Rambler grew up, production cars acquiring two cylinders in 1904 and four in 1906. Horizontally-opposed twins were made through 1909, but the fours (starting with Models 14, 15, and 16) superseded them. Unlike the twins with their two-speed epicyclic gearing, the fours had three-speed sliding-pinion gear-boxes, and either shaft or (in the case of the biggest) double side-chain drive. The

fours were conventional enough in most respects, but retained touches more reminiscent of European practice: detachable wheels were introduced in 1909 in place of the conventional detachable rims. The car shown, the 38 h.p. of 1912, was so equipped. Its engine was rather unusual at so late a date in having separately cast cylinders. A bigger engine, the 50 h.p. of 7·1 litres with dual ignition by coil and magneto, was also available. In 1913, over 10,000 cars were made, and in the same year, each new car was guaranteed for 10,000 miles. The name came to an end in 1913, the car being renamed Jeffery. Nash Motors, who took over the Thomas B. Jeffery Company, revived the name in 1957.

92 REX-SIMPLEX TYP C, 1913, 1912, Germany

The Hering und Richard concern of Ronneburg in Saxony began by making bicycle parts, progressed to motor-car components, and in 1901 started to make complete cars on French De Dion Bouton lines, using parts supplied by Cudell of Aachen, the German licence-holders for De Dion. After 1903 Rex-Simplex cars could be had with Fafnir engines as well. The biggest machine was a chain-driven four on Mercedes lines with Fafnir power unit. They went over to their own engines at the end of 1907. The Typ C 17/38 PS, which is shown here in 1912 and 1913 guise, was made from 1908 until 1914. It was a modern machine, with four cylinders cast in pairs, side valves in L-head formation, $4\frac{1}{2}$ litres, four forward speeds, and shaft drive. More from its quality than its design, the Rex-Simplex was known as the 'Mercedes from Ronneburg'. In 1911 it was used as the basis for a new range of Russo–Baltique cars (the only Russian passenger-car make to create any impression before 1914), which had previously been based on the Fondu from Belgium.

93 FIAT TIPO 51 ZERO,
1912, Italy

Until 1912, the Fiat was known as a large, powerful car (37) of fine quality and modern, if conventional design—by 1911 only the biggest in the range still used chain drive, and all models had L-head monobloc engines. From then on, however, the Fiat trend began to draw towards smaller machines aimed at a wider market. Of the three new models of 1912, Tipos 51, 52, and 53, the first and smallest (which is the car illustrated), also called the Tipo Zero, was the most popular, and was the first Fiat to sell in really large numbers, escaping from the make's 'luxury' image. This 1·8-litre machine, like its stablemates, had a four-cylinder side-valve engine and four forward speeds. Top speed was a creditable 50 m.p.h., and power output 19 b.h.p. at 2,000 r.p.m. The car was current until 1915.

94 MINERVA 16 h.p., 1912, Belgium

Like most budding motor manu-factureres, Sylvain de Jong started small, his 1900 offering being a twin-cylinder, chain-driven *voiturette*. From 1903, Minerva followed Belgian fashion in going over to big, powerful cars, initially designed largely according to the *système* Panhard apart from their mechanically-operated inlet valves—two, three, or four cylinders, of 10, 15, and 20 h.p., armoured-wood frames, and double side-chain drive. By then, the type was already retrograde, having been outclassed by the Mercedes from Germany, but instead of copying that car next, as did the majority of car-makers who favoured large, expensive machinery, Antwerp produced a more original machine. True, it had the four pair-cast cylinders, side valves in a T head, steel frame, honeycomb radiator and gate change of the current Mercedes, but this was now merely conventional. In the 1904 14-h.p. Minerva and its equally successful development the 16 h.p. of 1905, these features were combined with shaft drive in a medium-sized (three-litre), modestly-priced but exceedingly well-made car. The bigger 22-h.p. four that followed was in the same mould, though the 40-h.p. six was big (6 litres), fast, and costly. De Jong's next carefully considered exercise in originality un-veiled at the 1908 Brussels Salon, when the public were shown a 38 h.p. with Charles Yale Knight's double sleeve-valve engine, which, with the Coventry Daimler company, they were the first to introduce. By the end of 1909, only sleeve-valve Minervas were available—in 16-h.p., 26-h.p., and 38-h.p. form. They were current through 1910, 1911, and 1912. The vehicle shown is a 16 h.p. of 1912. It had a 2½-litre, four-cylinder engine (still bi-bloc), boasting all the quietness and smoothness of sleeve valves, dual ignition, four forward speeds, and worm final drive. These sleeve-valve Minervas were extremely strong and reliable, and could be made to go fast, as was shown by their triumph in the Austrian International Alpine Trials (a premier award in 1912, the prize of the Trieste Automobile Club in 1913, and a share in the Alpine Wander-Prize in 1914); in the Swedish Winter Trials (which Hans Osterman won in 1911, 1913, and 1914); and in their second, third, and fifth places in the 1914 Tourist Trophy Races. Even the middle-sized 26 h.p. could exceed 60 m.p.h. comfortably.

95 SPYKER, 1912, Holland

Jacobus and Hendrik Spyker were responsible for the only Dutch car that made an international name for itself until the coming of the DAF. This it did not only by means of the more orthodox qualities, but also through sensational technical ingenuity, not all of it successful commercially. Nothing of this was to be seen in the first car to emerge from the Trompenburg factory —the two-cylinder *voiturette* of 1900— nor in the 20-h.p. four that appeared in 1902, though this (like all Spykers) had shaft drive, which was unusual in a big car. 1903, however, saw two major innovations. The first had historical significance, in that Spyker became the first manufacturer (by a short head) to introduce a six-cylinder car—though it is true to say that others, particularly Napier, popularized the type. The second was a true *tour de force*, which set no trends either: a six-cylinder car with four-wheel drive and braking to all four wheels. A mere handful of

machines with this layout were made. Even the round-radiator vogue that Spyker helped to pioneer in 1905 was more closely associated with Hotchkiss and Delaunay-Belleville (53, 52). In 1909, some Spykers with pneumatic transmission were built. The scene-stealers overshadowed the modern, refined, reliable cars, incorporating original but practical ideas, that made up the bulk of the range. From 1903 to 1910, the chassis side members were extended to form the base of the crank-case and gear-box, creating an under-tray that kept dust out of the machinery (and helped to lay it), and also made for a very rigid structure. In 1910 this feature was dropped, but a remarkable new engine was introduced on some models. It had two worm-driven trans-verse camshafts, each driving both inlet and exhaust valves, and unit con-struction of engine and gear-box. This design was a success technically, as it resulted in great smoothness and silence of running, but it was not economic. The new car was sold in four-cylinder form, but an experimental twin was also made, and is illustrated here.

96 STELLA 20/30 CV, 1912, Switzerland

In 1901, the Compagnie de l'Industrie Electrique et Mécanique (C.I.E.M.), who had made electric motors and equipment, started building the former (and also gasoline engines) for motor vehicles. Three years later, C.I.E.M. began to make complete cars, each fitted with both an electric motor and a gasoline engine. At higher road speeds when the engine load was not great, a dynamo on the drive shaft between the engine and the gear-box operated as a generator, charging the batteries. When the engine was under load, as when climbing a hill, the dynamo automatically functioned as an electric motor auxiliary to the engine. Heavy commercial vehicles, powered solely by electricity, were also made. These retained the C.I.E.M. name when, in 1906, the passenger cars were renamed Stella and became conventional, though modern and very handsome. They had four vertical cylinders in line, cast monobloc from 1910, with side valves in an L head, three or four forward speeds, and shaft drive. The 20/30 CV of 1912 that is illustrated was the biggest in the range of three then current, with a 90 × 160 mm. engine giving four litres, and a four-speed gear-box. Production ended in 1913, when 200 vehicles of all types had been made.

INDEX

Make	Model	Ref. No. (colour)	Page No. description
Ford	Model T	47	133
Franklin	Model D	73	146
Gaggenau	Typ D 10-18, Typ 60	35	127
Germain	18/22 h.p.	38	128
Gräf und Stift	18/32 PS	78	149
H.L.	10/15 CV, 12/18 CV	83	152
Hotchkiss	Type T	53	137
Humber	8 h.p.	41	130
I.H.C.	1907	22	120
Iris	15 h.p.	87	153
Itala	35/45 h.p.	25	122
Jowett	1911	70	145
K.R.I.T.	25/30 h.p.	90	155
Lanchester	20 h.p.	30	124
Lancia	Tipo 51 Alfa	36	128
Laurin-Klément	Type B	24	121
Le Zèbre	4 CV	64	142
Martini	12/16 CV	51	136
Mass	8 CV	3	110
Maxwell	Model HB, Model A	23	121
Mercedes	35/40 PS	10	113
Métallurgique	12 CV	63	142
Minerva	16 h.p.	94	157
Morris-Oxford	1913	89	155
Mors	Type R	1	109
NAG	20/24 PS	11	114
Napier	45 h.p., 40 h.p.	20	119
New Eagle	1907, 1908	19	118
Opel	4/8 PS	50	135
Opel	6/16 PS	77	149

Make	Model	Ref. No. (colour)	Page No. (description)
Panhard–Levassor	15 CV	82	151
Peerless	35 h.p., 24 h.p.	9	113
Peugeot	16 h.p. Type 116, 7/9 h.p. Type 125	27	123
Phänomobil	4/6 PS	61	141
Piccolo	5 PS	15	116
Pierce Great Arrow	28 h.p.	8	112
Premier	40 h.p.	49	135
Rambler	38 h.p.	91	156
Renault	20/30 CV	12	114
Renault	Model AX	40	129
Rex-Simplex	Typ C	92	156
Riley	10 h.p.	44	131
Rochet-Schneider	25 CV	67	144
Rolls-Royce	15 h.p.	6	111
Rolls-Royce	40/50 h.p.	17	117
Rover	Twelve	86	153
Scania	18/20 h.p., 18/24 h.p.	80	150
Schacht	1908	32	125
Schneider TH	18 CV	84	152
Spyker	1912	95	158
Standard	30 h.p., 40 h.p.	18	118
Stanley	10 h.p.	76	148
Stearns	45/90 h.p.	34	126
Stella	20/30 CV	96	158
Stoewer	Typ B6, Typ C1	60	140
Sunbeam	12/16 h.p.	88	154
Thomas Flyer	Model 6-70	21	120
Tribelhorn	Victoria, Phaeton	26	122
Turcat-Méry	18 CV	65	143
Valveless	25 h.p.	56	138
Vauxhall	9 h.p.	4	110
Vauxhall	12/16 h.p.	46	132
White	30 h.p.	33	126
Wolseley	16/20 h.p.	68	144